I was so deeply touched to have ⎽⎽ ⎽⎽ ⎽⎽ ⎽⎽ ⎽⎽ ⎽⎽ shape my prayer life. Cindy Mallin has done a master⎽⎽ ⎽⎽ of combining the inspiration of a spiritual giant with practical questions of application. This book could transform your relationship with God!

—Dr. Joel C. Hunter, Senior Pastor
Northland—A Church Distributed, Longwood, Florida

What a gift to Christians! Sometimes we forget the simple things like God being in charge of our lives and faithful all the time. This book looks at George Mueller and reminds us of the absolute sufficiency of God. Mueller was not very different than we are, and God will be just as faithful and sufficient for us as he was for Mueller. Read this book and you'll "rise up and call me blessed" for recommending it to you.

—Dr. Steve Brown, Professor
Reformed Theological Seminary, Orlando, Florida
Author and Founder and President of Key Life Network

George Mueller was an amazing man, and Cindy Mallin has captured his heart on paper. I highly recommend this book to anyone who wants to be challenged in his or her prayer life and walk of faith with Jesus. As a pastor, I want to be challenged in my personal prayer life, and I am always looking for ways to encourage those in our church to pray. I am going to encourage every person in our church to read this book.

—Rick Rohlin, Senior Pastor
Praise Fellowship, Russell, Pennsylvania

Cindy Mallin in her book *Simple Trust, Simple Prayers* opens our eyes to the faith-filled life of George Mueller. Mueller's journal entries show how we too can tap into God's power: by praying expectantly for God to meet our daily needs.

—DR. DON WILSON, SENIOR PASTOR
CHRIST'S CHURCH OF THE VALLEY, PEORIA, ARIZONA

George Mueller is one of those rare men whose lives demonstrate consistent faith and dependence upon God. In the face of great trial, when all hope seems lost, even up to the final hour, George Mueller can be seen on his knees in prayer. Through his journals, Cindy Mallin has captured the essence of Mueller's heart. It's an inspiring read for those who want to have their faith in God strengthened.

—JASON FRITZ, PASTOR
HIGHLANDS CHURCH, SCOTTSDALE, ARIZONA

In this book, Cindy Mallin unleashes a powerful rendering of George Mueller's journal regarding his journey of learning to simply trust the faithfulness of God through prayer. In taking us deeper by asking probing questions and challenging us to ask the "what ifs" in our own lives, Cindy provides a way for each of us to experience the power of prayer. The impact of prayer to change lives is a message that encourages every reader.

—TERI MELLO, PROFESSIONAL CERTIFIED COACH,
FOOTSTEPS LIFE COACHING
BIBLE STUDY TEACHER AND SPEAKER, CHANDLER, ARIZONA

George Mueller is known and admired by many Christians. Reading his journal reveals how amazing our Lord is in watching over His people. Cindy Mallin challenges us to not only read this wonderful man's story but also apply the faith principles to our own lives. Thank you, Cindy!

—REV. SAM CLARKE, DIRECTOR
GATEWAY TO ISRAEL MINISTRIES, FRANKLIN, TENNESSEE

SIMPLE TRUST
SIMPLE PRAYERS

SIMPLE TRUST SIMPLE PRAYERS

CINDY MALLIN

CREATION
HOUSE

SIMPLE TRUST, SIMPLE PRAYERS by Cindy Mallin
Published by Creation House
A Charisma Media Company
600 Rinehart Road
Lake Mary, Florida 32746
www.charismamedia.com

All Scripture quotations are from the Holy Bible, New International Version. Copyright © 1973, 1978, 1984, International Bible Society. Used by permission.

Based on author's discussion and paraphrasing of George Mueller's *Answers to Prayer* (Chicago, IL: Moody Publishers, 1984).

Design Director: Bill Johnson
Cover design by Nathan Morgan

www.cindymallin.com

Library of Congress Control Number: 2010939120
International Standard Book Number: 978-1-61638-275-9

17 18 19 20 21 — 9 8 7 6 5
Printed in the United States of America

This book would never have been written if it weren't for my beloved husband, Mickey. He is my encourager, supporter, proofreader, prayer partner, business partner, and truly my rock. He believes in me and in the power of the written word. And he makes me laugh every day!

Mickey, this book is dedicated to you.

In all my Christian life (now sixty-nine years), never once did God fail to direct me if I carefully read the Word of God and sincerely and patiently sought to know His will by the teaching of the Holy Spirit. On the other hand, if I did not have honesty of heart and uprightness before God, or if I did not patiently wait on God for instruction, or if I preferred the counsel of people to what God tells me in the Bible, I made great mistakes.

—GEORGE MUELLER, MARCH 1895

CONTENTS

ACKNOWLEDGMENTS

THE IDEA FOR this book began in an unusual way. A few months before we were married, Mickey and I began what quickly became one of our favorite pastimes—reading good books aloud to each other. Mickey is Jewish and had come to Christ a year before we married. Since he had no Christian background at all, I tried to remember some of the great, classic books I had read many years before that taught me about faith.

One book that forever changed my life was a book by George Mueller, and I located a copy on the Internet. I was so excited to share Mueller's story with my husband! We quickly discovered, however, that we had a major problem. I read one short paragraph, and Mickey stopped me. "I have absolutely no idea what you just read," he said. We realized that the more formal language used in the 1800's no longer made sense to today's reader. And so I spontaneously paraphrased what I had just read and resumed reading the next paragraph. He stopped me again, and I paraphrased again.

The story itself was so compelling, however, that somewhere along the way we decided it was too good to let it die on dusty bookshelves. Thus was born the idea to paraphrase and publish this book.

Thank you, Mickey! If it wasn't for you, this book would never have been written.

No book is ever written without the inspiration, assistance, and encouragement of many others. Some of them deserve mention here.

My daughter, Monica Briggs, inspires me with her straight-forward faith. Her life has not been simple; yet today as she lives the challenging life of a single mom, she continues to learn what it means to trust God. She is still teaching me. She read the early manuscript, encouraged me, and prayed. Thanks, Monica.

Linda Patrick, my good friend and prayer partner, is a constant source of encouragement to me and to so many others. Thank you, Linda.

My sister, Kathy Mannara, was a strong supporter and encourager from the time she heard of the book. She took the early manuscript to her own church in Phoenix and used it to teach a class there. Thanks, Kath!

Barbara Olsen, Director of Adult Equipping at Northland Church in Longwood, Florida, was more instrumental than she knows. Barb is the person we approached with our initial idea to use this manuscript to teach a Sunday morning class, and it was her great enthusiasm that propelled us at that point. It was Barb who suggested including discussion questions for each chapter. Thank you, Barb!

Members of that first class began to pray for this book to find a publisher. As week by week we saw how each chapter challenged and impacted lives, we were encouraged. Thank you Lynn Kern, Anne Moore, Jane Browning, Jim and Linda Patrick, Jamila "J" Millette, Paula Bauer, Frank Mannina, Bob and Linda Schwalbe, Jayne Sims, Margarete Sampson, Linda San Souci Filegar, Colette DeFilippo, Mark and Phyllis Chen, Carol Speich, and Denise Worthen.

And last but not least, members of our home group prayed for this book from beginning to end. Thank you Jim and Linda Patrick, Melissa Holt, Bill and Kim Hulme, Glenn and Linda Jedlicka, and Tim Carroll.

Most of all, thank you to Jesus my Lord! To God be the glory! Before I even knew Him, God loved me. He cared enough to send His one and only Son, Jesus, to the cross as my substitute. Thank you, heavenly Father!

INTRODUCTION

Things looked bleak for the children of George Mueller's orphanage in England. It was time for breakfast, and there was no food. In the dining room long tables were set with empty plates and empty mugs. Not only was there no food in the kitchen, there was no money to buy any.

A little girl, whose father was a friend of Mueller's, was visiting in the home. Mueller took her hand and said, "Come and see what our Father will do."

And then he did what he always did when it was mealtime—he prayed.

"Dear Father, we thank You for what You are going to give us to eat."

Immediately they heard a knock at the door. When they opened it, there stood the local baker. "Mr. Mueller," he said, "I couldn't sleep last night. Somehow I had a feeling you had no bread for breakfast, so I got up at 2 a.m. and baked some fresh bread. Here it is." Mueller thanked him and gave praise to God.

A few minutes later, there was a second knock. It was the milkman. His cart had broken down in front of the orphanage. He said that rather than let the milk spoil, he would like to give it to the children.[1]

STORIES LIKE THIS teach us what it means to pray and trust God to answer. But this isn't just a story meant to touch our hearts. It is just another day in George Mueller's life.

Even mature, committed followers of Christ sometimes need to be challenged. It is our nature to compare ourselves with others—a recipe for mediocrity if I ever heard one! Let's face it—most believers live lives of mediocrity; and if we are measuring ourselves by comparing ourselves with mediocrity, what is to challenge us?

Case in point: If you've been in the church for very long, you know a lot about prayer. At least you think you do.

But in your more honest moments, you also know that prayer is sometimes boring, which you don't admit because you also know how important it is—or is *supposed* to be.

The truth is, prayer is one of those mysteries of the faith that we never quite master. Throughout the centuries very few people have ever arrived at a comfortable place regarding their own private, personal prayer life. Rarely do we see what it looks like when someone lives a life in total trust, praying for basic, daily needs and actually believing that God will answer.

I want you to meet George Mueller.

Mueller lived in England in the 1800s; his life and story are still well-known among seasoned, well-read Christians. But for the generation of readers who would never touch the King James Version of the Bible because it makes no sense to them, Mueller's writings have been lost in the dust pile along with other classic literature.

This book is an all-new, paraphrased edition of highlights from Mueller's journals. You'll learn how his dream of establishing and operating orphanages all began. You may wonder at Mueller's decision to trust solely in God for every need and never tell a single person what those needs might be. You'll walk through some dark days with Mueller. You'll laugh; you'll cry. Sometimes you'll dance with joy! You may gasp—*often!*

More than another thoughtful essay on prayer, this is simple eavesdropping into one man's daily journal entries. Mueller occasionally turns aside and records some advice aimed directly at us, the readers; but mostly he just writes the daily events of his life. He doesn't tell us how to pray; he lets us watch his life—over seven decades! This is not a passing phase for Mueller.

What does it mean to pray and trust God to answer?

I never knew. Somehow I had missed it. Until I saw what trusting God looked like in Mueller's life, I didn't really know what it meant. What I learned changed my life forever.

> And my God will meet all your needs according
> to his glorious riches in Christ Jesus.
> —PHILIPPIANS 4:19

What would happen if *you* decided to really believe God?

WARNING: READING THIS BOOK WILL CHANGE YOUR LIFE. PROCEED AT YOUR OWN RISK.

Author's note: All references to English currency (pounds, shillings, pence, etc.) have been converted into approximate values for American dollars. However, no attempt has been made to factor in inflation because inflation (and/or deflation) rates can vary over time. For approximate conversion to the year 2010, take the dollar values shown in the book and multiply by a factor of twenty-five. So if you read of Mueller receiving ten dollars, in 2010 terms that would be about $250. At the end of his life, you will note that the total of his worldly possessions was eight hundred dollars (equivalent to twenty thousand dollars in 2010), but throughout his lifetime, he had handled more than $8 million ($200 million in 2010).

Chapter 1

ORPHANAGE? WHAT
WAS HE THINKING?

*G*EORGE *M*UELLER *IS well-known as the founder of several orphanages in England. These orphanages became known as great monuments to a prayer-answering God. Mr. Mueller clearly states why he established these orphanages.*

FEARFUL OLDER CHRISTIANS

I noticed that many older Christians were consumed with fear of going to the poorhouse, because if their health failed, they might become unable to work any longer. If I reminded them how their heavenly Father has always helped those who put their trust in Him, sometimes they said that times have changed. I saw clearly that these children of God did not look upon God as the *living* God.

My spirit was very saddened by this and I longed to find a way to encourage these children of God. I wanted to find a way to show them clearly that God does not forsake those who rely on Him—even in changing times.

BUSINESS PEOPLE

I also noticed how common it was for Christian business people to suffer with guilty consciences because in business they behaved just like unbelievers—engaging in unethical, immoral, and dishonest business practices. These Christians seemed to believe there was no other way to succeed in business, and I was grieved to see how guilt-ridden they were. These people pointed to the need to remain competitive and the pressures of the world's economy as reasons why their business could not succeed if the business was conducted according to the Bible.

I was amazed that these people even expressed the wish that it might be different, but seemed resigned to the "fact" that it must be so; business is business, and compromises must be made to succeed. Very rarely did I see anyone make a stand for God with a holy determination to trust in the living God, depend on Him, and maintain a good conscience.

To the business people, likewise, I wanted to find a visible way to show that God does not change, and that He can still be depended upon in business.

EMPLOYEES IN QUESTIONABLE, COMPROMISING EMPLOYMENT

I also wanted to find a way to address this third group of people. It grieved my heart to see people who seemed to feel caught in jobs where their consciences were violated. They were afraid to make a move to leave their jobs because they were afraid of losing their paychecks. They were, in effect, choosing their paychecks over choosing to put their faith in a living God.

I longed to find a way to strengthen their faith by giving them not only selected sections of the Word of God that showed His willingness and ability to help everyone who relies on Him, but also to show them *proof* that He is the same today. I knew very well that the Word of God ought to be enough (and it was, by grace, enough for me); but still, I longed to find a way to help my brothers and sisters in the faith. I wanted them to see by some visible proof that the faithfulness of the Lord has not changed through the years or centuries.

I remembered what a great blessing it was to me to learn

about God's great servant, A. H. Franke, who, in complete dependence upon the living God, established an immense orphanage in 1695. I had visited this orphanage several times and saw what God had done there.

I began to realize that I was bound to be a servant of the church of God, and to live in such a way as to demonstrate a life of taking God at His Word and relying wholly upon it. This dawning realization grew from my own awareness that so many believers were harassed and distressed, or feeling guilty because they were not trusting in God. I realized that God was using this awareness to awaken in my heart the desire to set before the church (and before the world) concrete, visible proof that He has not changed at all.

With this goal in mind—demonstrating God's unchanging nature and His willingness to answer prayer—establishing an orphanage seemed like the best way to demonstrate this proof. It had to be something that could be seen at a glance.

Now if I, a poor man, could open and operate an orphanage purely by prayer and faith without ever asking any individual for help, it seemed to me that this tangible demonstration of God's blessing would strengthen the faith of God's children, besides showing unbelievers that we serve a God who can be trusted.

This, then, was the primary reason for establishing the orphanage. To be sure, I did truly want God to use me to care for orphans, and I also really wanted the opportunity to lead them to faith in Christ; but still, the first and primary objective was (and still is) that God might be glorified by the fact that the orphans under my care would have all their needs met using *only* prayer and faith, without me or my colleagues ever asking *anyone* for funds or supplies. I wanted people to see that God is still faithful. The living God still hears and answers prayer.

I can now see that I was not mistaken; God's faithfulness has been abundantly proven since November 1835—both by the number of unbelievers who have come to trust Christ because

3

of this project, and also by the stories of believers who have been encouraged in their faith to pray and trust God themselves. I give all glory and honor to God. I am truly grateful that He has enabled me to serve Him in this way.

TALK ABOUT THIS

1. In your own words: Why did Mueller establish the orphanages?

2. Your own observation: Are people the same today as in the 1800s, when he wrote the book?

3. Read Appendix B "How to Know God's Will—the Mueller Method." What does he say is 90 percent of the problem? Do you agree or disagree? Why?

4. Read Appendix C "Reading the Bible Cover to Cover." How important is Bible reading to Mueller? Why?

APPLICATION: WHAT IF I...?

1. What if I resolved to follow God's will, no matter what it was?

2. What if I read from the Bible every single day?

3. What if my goal in life was to demonstrate God's unchanging nature and His willingness to answer prayer?

Chapter 2

HOW IT ALL BEGAN—
THE EARLY DAYS

NOVEMBER 16, 1835: Lately, the idea of establishing an orphanage for the city of Bristol and depending on the Lord is always on my mind. I have been praying in earnest for two weeks now, asking God if this idea is really from Him, that He would bring it about; but if not, that He would remove all thoughts of it from my mind.

My uncertainty about knowing the Lord's mind did not come from questioning whether it would be pleasing in His sight. I knew there should be a home and Bible education for homeless children. Rather my uncertainty was whether it was His will or not that I should be the instrument. My plate was already very full, and I did not want to embark on such an enormous project without clearly knowing that it was His will, and that He wanted me to be the one to bring it about.

I took comfort in knowing that if it were His will, He would provide not only the finances but also the staff to take care of the children. I knew that my part of the work would take only a portion of my time, but I wanted to be ready for whatever might be required. The whole two weeks I spent praying about this, I never asked the Lord for money or for people.

December 5, 1835: Today, however, my prayers became very different. I was reading Psalm 81 and was struck with verse 10: "Open wide your mouth and I will fill it." I had never had this verse strike me before, and now it seemed to jump out at me. I thought about these words for several minutes, wondering why God might be stopping me right here.

I then clearly felt that I was supposed to apply these words to the orphanage. That's when I realized that I had not yet asked God for anything for it except to know His will and whether I should even do it. I fell on my knees and opened my mouth wide, asking Him for much. I asked in submission to His will and did not fix a deadline for Him to answer my prayer.

I prayed that He would give me a house (either as a loan, or as an outright gift, or that someone might pay the rent for a house). I also asked God for $5,000 and for suitable people to care for the children. Later I asked the Lord to nudge the hearts of His people to send me furniture for the house and clothes for the children.

As I was praying for these specific needs, I was fully aware of what I was doing—I was asking for things that I had absolutely no means of obtaining on my own, and no one I knew did either. I also knew that none of this was too much for the Lord to provide.

December 10, 1835—five days later: This morning I received a letter from a couple:

> We would like to apply for service at the orphanage. We would also like to give the orphanage all the furniture we have (since we know it is the Lord who gave it to us and it is for His use). We would like to do this without receiving any salary at all because we trust that if it is God's will to place us there, He will supply all our needs.

December 13, 1835—three days later: Today a friend told me he was going to give us $1 per week, or $52 a year, as long as the Lord gives him the means. He gave me $2 as payment for his first two weeks. Later today another couple asked if they could work at the orphanage for no salary. They also wanted to bring all the furniture they had with them.

NEEDING ENCOURAGEMENT

December 17, 1835—four days later: I was rather downcast last night and again this morning about the whole orphanage idea. I questioned whether I should even be doing it, so I asked the Lord to give me some encouragement.

Soon after this prayer, a friend sent me thirty yards of various fabric suitable for children's clothing. And then this evening another friend brought a laundry drying rack, three dresses, four aprons, six handkerchiefs, three quilts, one blanket, two salt shakers, six tin cups, and six teaspoons. He also brought $1 that had been given to him by three different individuals. He told me that he would send an additional $500 tomorrow.

BUT WHERE ARE THE CHILDREN?

A notice was sent to the press announcing the opening of the girls' orphanage and our proposal to establish another orphanage for infants. As far as I remember, I have brought even the minutest details before the Lord in prayer. I am conscious of my own weakness and ignorance.

I now realized that there was one point I had never prayed about—that the Lord would send children. I had taken for granted there would be plenty of children. Indeed, I expected there would soon be a waiting list of children wanting to be admitted into the orphanage.

However, the closer we came to opening day, the more I began to secretly wonder if God might disappoint me. Perhaps He wanted to show me a bigger lesson—that I would not prosper in a single thing unless I first brought it to Him in prayer.

Sure enough, opening day came and we had not received even a single application! Opening day, and *not* a single child!

Prior to this day, I had often wondered whether I might have been mistaken about the whole project. Had I misunderstood God's leading altogether?

This was a heavy burden for me, and I went before my God in prayer the whole evening of February 3 to examine my heart once again. I asked God to search my heart to see if my motives were pure. Was it really my main goal to glorify God? Could this project demonstrate to a watching world that it is indeed not a mistake to trust in the living God?

I wanted to be clear before God that the primary motive of my heart was to glorify God; my secondary motive was for the spiritual welfare of the children; and thirdly, I wanted to care for the children's physical needs. Knowing how my own selfish needs can so easily deceive, I laid low before God for some time.

At last I was peaceful, and knew clearly that God would be glorified in all of this, even if that meant the entire project came to *nothing*! My heart rejoiced, knowing that God was indeed in charge.

And now, I continued to sense that God did plan for this orphanage. I could now ask heartily for Him to send us children. My heart was now very peaceful and more assured than ever that God Himself would do it.

February 4, 1836: This very next day the first application arrived, and since then forty-two more have come in.

Up and Running

June 15, 1837: Today I focused again on earnest prayer because we need a total of $5,000. Much of it has now been received, but we need to have the complete amount. This evening $25 was received, making the whole $5,000 complete.

I want to repeat and emphasize this very important fact: all of this money, each item of clothing, every piece of furniture that has come in has come without a *single request* for a *single thing*. To God be the glory!

JUST FOR TODAY

July 22, 1838: By this time, there are nearly 100 people to care for and we only have about $100 in hand.

This evening I was walking in our little garden, meditating on Hebrews 13:8, "Jesus Christ is the same yesterday and today and forever." While meditating on His unchangeable love, power, and wisdom, and turning it all into prayer about myself and applying His unchangeable love, power, and wisdom both to my current spiritual and earthly circumstances, all at once I thought of the current needs of the orphanage. Immediately I thought, *In His love and power, Jesus has always supplied me with everything I needed for the orphans; in His same unchangeable love and power, He will provide me with everything needed for the future.*

Joy began to flow through me as I thought about the unchangeableness of our incredible Lord. About one minute later, a letter was brought to me with $100 enclosed. The accompanying note said, "Please use this money in any way you deem best for the needs of the orphans. It is not a large sum, but it may be sufficient for today's needs. I trust that God will show you how it is to be used."

The Lord usually provides for one day's needs at a time; tomorrow brings its own needs, and the Lord provides for them then. Of this $100, I used $50 for the orphan fund and $50 for other items, and was, therefore, able to meet the expenses that I knew were coming due in the next four days.

WAITING, WAITING

November 21, 1838: Never were we so broke as we are today. Our funds are nearly depleted. Nevertheless, there was a good dinner, and by helping one another with bread, etc., we knew we would get through the day. However, none of the houses had food for the following day.

After prayer, when I left for the day, I told the staff that we must wait upon God for help and see how He would deliver us this time. I was sure that God would provide; but at the moment, we were indeed destitute.

When I arrived at Kingsdown, I felt like I needed more exercise so I took the long way home and walked by Clarence Place. About twenty yards from my home, I met a friend who walked with me and after a little conversation he gave me $50 to be used for coal, blankets, and warm clothing. He also gave me $25 for the orphans and $25 for the Bible school. Apparently, this friend had stopped by twice while I was away, and if I had been *thirty seconds* later, I would have missed him. But the Lord knew our need for this very time, and apparently He had directed me to take the longer walk home so as to meet this friend.

No Disappointment

September 21, 1840: It is Monday, and we have more than enough in hand for today and tomorrow. Today a visiting friend from London gave me $50 to be used as needed. Since we have been praying for the needs of the Bible school and for missionary support, I used it for them. This friend knew nothing about our work when he arrived three days ago.

So I see how God shows His continued care over us by raising up new sources of help. They that trust in the Lord shall never be confounded! Some who may be regular supporters may die, others may fall away from serving God, some may decide to send their donations elsewhere, and still others may no longer have the means to send at all. But I see now that none of that matters—I see how God is able to raise up new supporters, thus keeping us always supplied with everything we need. I began to see that if we ever made the mistake of depending on certain *people* for our needs, we would surely be disappointed. Instead, I saw that we were to lean on the *living God* alone. If we did this, we would be beyond disappointment, beyond being forsaken because of a donor's death or lack of means or change of heart, or because a supporter lost his job.

How precious it is to have learned this lesson! To stand with God alone in this work, and yet to be happy and know that surely no good thing will be withheld from us as we walk uprightly!

TALK ABOUT THIS

1. Mueller was in the practice of reading through the Bible. When he came to Psalm 81, a verse jumped out at him. Have you ever had a verse speak to you when you were reading the Bible? Share.

2. "I took comfort in knowing that if it were His will, He would provide not only the finances, but also the staff." Do you have this peace when you move forward with your projects? Share.

3. Because Mueller prayed for very specific things, he was able to "connect the dots" and recognize when God answered. Do you think we ever miss seeing what God is doing? Is that because of the way we pray?

4. "As far as I remember, I have brought even the minutest details before the Lord in prayer. I am conscious of my own weakness and ignorance." Do you think we are very aware of our own weakness and ignorance? How does this affect the way we pray?

5. "I began to see that if we ever made the mistake of depending on certain *people* for our needs, we would surely be disappointed." Do most people (including Christians) depend on their employer

(paycheck) for their needs? What do you think Mueller would say about that?

APPLICATION: WHAT IF I...?

1. What if I had a project to demonstrate God's faithfulness? What would that be? How would I begin?

2. What if I always read from the Bible before I began praying? Would this change my prayers? How?

3. What if I made my prayers more specific? Would I see the hand of God in response?

4. What if I became aware of my own weakness and ignorance? How would that change anything for me?

Chapter 3

PRAYERS AND ANSWERS—
DOES THIS MEAN
SMOOTH SAILING?

Editor's note: The following is part of Mueller's annual review for the year 1841.

DURING THIS YEAR I learned of the conversion of one of the very greatest sinners I've ever heard of in my entire life. I had often prayed with his wife and asked the Lord for his conversion. This dear woman had suffered great distress because of her husband's cruel hatred toward her. He was not able to provoke her to lash out at him, and that seemed to fuel his rage toward her even more. We recognized that this was suffering for Jesus' sake, and had repeatedly prayed for this man's conversion to Christ.

When it was at its worst, I pleaded with God using the promise of Matthew 18:19: "Again, I tell you that if two of you on earth agree about anything you ask for, it will be done for you by my Father in heaven." And now, praise God, it is done! This rage-filled man is converted.

SPIRITUAL GROWTH

On May 25 I began to ask the Lord to work powerfully among the believers who work with us in Bristol. I asked God to bring them greater genuine spirituality than they have ever had before, and now I am joyfully recording that truly He has answered this request! All praise goes to our great God! There has never been a time when I have seen more grace, truth, and spiritual power among us. Not that we have arrived; we are keenly aware that we must press on; we are still far, far from the goal. But the Lord has been very good to us, and we are celebrating with great thanksgiving.

WITHHOLDING THE ANNUAL REPORT

December 9, 1841: Today I received $3. We are now nearing the end of the sixth year of the work, and have on hand only the rent money, and still I recognize that during this entire year we have been supplied with everything we needed.

During the last three years we closed our accounting books on this date, and then held public meetings for the benefit of interested parties. We always reported how the Lord had supplied our needs for the year, and we always printed a summary report for distribution to supporters and anyone interested.

This year, however, it seemed better to delay both the public meetings and the printed report. Here's why: We had learned how all-important it was to lean entirely upon the Lord for all our needs. Our faith was built on an agreement that we would never speak about or write a single word about the needs of the work. We agreed that we would trust in God alone to meet all of our needs. We felt that if we ever violated this agreement, we would no longer be assured of God's provision. And so, we were content to continue trusting God.

The purpose of the public meetings and the printed reports had never been to expose our neediness or to manipulate the emotions of the recipients in an attempt to receive more donations. We were clear about that. The intent was simply to convey stories about the orphanages, tell how trustworthy God always was, and therefore, to encourage others to trust God.

It seemed to me that if we held the public meeting and printed our report at this time, it might appear to some that we were looking for donations. Because the need was so great at this time, our report could possibly be seen as an attempt to manipulate emotions and secure donations. We wanted to avoid any possible perceptions that we might have ulterior motives.

With this in mind, we decided that in the midst of our current deep poverty, we would continue to depend upon the living God alone, and therefore, delay the public reporting of our current dire circumstances. This seemed to be the perfect way to demonstrate the truth of our trust. If it were otherwise, we might have been glad that the time for issuing the annual report was upon us!

We went quietly about our work for some time, without saying anything. We reviewed our primary purpose for this entire work: it was not primarily for the benefit of the orphans (as much as we truly cared for them). Rather we renewed our commitment that the primary purpose was to demonstrate *how utterly faithful God is*, for the benefit of believers whose faith is weak.

The public meetings and the printed reports were both delayed for several months. The decision was made not to expose our poverty. Even in the midst of dire circumstances, we felt clear that publicizing our poverty would have devastated our work. We were peaceful.

December 18, 1841—nine days later: Saturday morning—I am now at the hour of greatest need; I have only four pennies in hand (which I found in the box at my house). Still, I fully believe the Lord will supply us this day with whatever we need.

I want to emphasize two things: (1) Our delaying of the public meetings and reports was done for God, but also, (2) God's way always leads into trial as far as sight and sense are concerned. Nature will always be tried in God's ways. The Lord was saying by this poverty, "I will now see whether you truly lean upon Me and whether you truly look to Me."

Of all the seasons I had ever passed through since beginning this faith walk up to that time, my faith had never been tested as much as during these four months. And even now it would have been possible to change our minds regarding the timing of these annual reports because no one knew about any of this. In fact, we knew that many believers looked forward to receiving these reports with delight.

In the end, the Lord continues to hold us steady and we continue to follow Him.

HE IS ALWAYS FAITHFUL

January 25, 1842—one month later: Perhaps the reader may wonder what would happen if we ever really did run out of funds, food, or supplies for the children. What would we do if meal time arrived and there was no food?

My heart is clear: this absolutely *could* happen, for I know how deceitful our hearts are. If we should ever go off on our own, if we should ever cease to depend solely on the living God, or if we should live with unrepentant and unconfessed sin, then this is exactly what would, in fact, occur.

But as long as we keep our eyes on Jesus and *trust in Him alone* to meet our needs, and as long as we confess any sin as soon as we know of it, if we truly repent and are determined to live life God's way, then such a thing *cannot* occur.

Dear Reader, if you yourself walk with God and if His glory is dear to you, I urge you to pray for us, for how awful would be the disgrace brought upon His holy name if we, who have so publicly made our claims that He is always faithful, should in the end bring disgrace to Him—either by unbelief in the hour of trial or by a life of sin in the end.

DELAYED BUT SURE

March 9, 1842—six weeks later: At a time of greatest need, both for the Bible schools and the orphanages, I knew that we could not go on without help from somewhere. And at the exact time of this need, I received $50 from a man who lives near Dublin. I split the money between the Bible schools and the orphanages.

I took note that at this time of great need, my soul was truly waiting upon the Lord. I was on the watch for any arrival of supplies throughout the morning. However, the mail arrived and nothing came. This did not discourage me in the least. I reminded myself that the Lord can send money and supplies without using the mail system. God has no limits on how He can work.

Not long after, I received the $50. This donation had been sent to the boys' orphanage and the staff then sent it over to me.

LIKE A FATHER

March 17, 1842—eight days later: From the twelfth to the sixteenth we received $22 for the orphans. We have been in a state of perpetual poverty for several months now, and our needs were exceedingly great. I left my house a few minutes before seven to walk to the orphanages. I wanted to see if there was money enough to pay for the delivery of milk, which is usually delivered about 8 a.m. On the way I prayed specifically that the Lord would not lay on us more burden than we would be able to bear, and that He would refresh and renew our faith by sending us help.

As I prayed, I reminded God that people were watching this whole faith-supported project (both believers and unbelievers), and what it would look like to them if we had to close down the orphanages because of a lack of funds; therefore, He would not permit this to happen. I confessed my own unworthiness to be used of God in this endeavor.

While I was still walking and engaged in this prayer, I met a man who was walking to his place of business. We exchanged greetings and continued on our own ways. Suddenly he turned around and ran back after me, extending his hand with $5 for the orphans. The Lord had speedily answered my prayer!

Truly it is worth it to be poor and be greatly tried in faith if it means seeing how faithful God is day by day. It is not possible for our heavenly Father to do otherwise. He has already given us the greatest proof possible that He loves us—He gave us His own Son! Surely He will also freely give us all things.

TRUSTING IN THE LORD VS. TRUSTING IN PEOPLE

May 6, 1845: About six weeks ago, a man implied that he was expecting a considerable sum of money, and that he planned to give $500 of it to me for the orphanage, plus some additional funds for my own personal expenses. However, day after day passed, and the money did not arrive. I knew better than to trust in this money, and yet, we were very, very needy at the time. I kept thinking about this man's promise, but continued to be thankful for God's grace that kept me from trusting in this *man*. I continued to trust only in the *Lord* to meet our needs.

Week after week passed and this money did not come. Suddenly this morning I realized there was value in this. I began to realize that I should absolutely never place any value at all in a person's promise, because I might easily be diverted from my intention of trusting and valuing God and God alone. I saw that such promises could begin to consume my thoughts, and I might turn toward such a person for funds; and that would mean I would turn away from God. I finally saw that I must never divert my focus; God must remain my singular focus.

Therefore, when it came time for my usual prayer time with my wife, I prayed about the work that was placed in my hands and asked God to completely remove from my mind thoughts of the promised funds from this man. I wanted to treat it as if it were worth not even one cent. The only thing that was worth anything was what came to me from God Himself.

My wife and I had not quite finished praying when the mail was delivered and included this letter:

> May 5, 1845
>
> Beloved Brother,
>
> Are you still banking at Stuckey & Company at Bristol? Please confirm at your earliest convenience, as I wish to deposit $350 in your account. This sum should be used as the Lord gives you wisdom. I shall wait to hear from you before proceeding.
>
> Ever affectionately yours,
>
> (name withheld)

Thus the Lord rewarded my wife and me in our determination not to look to any particular person for our needs but to God alone.

But this was not the end of it. About 2:00 p.m. I received $835 of the long-ago promised funds from this man. Apparently he had just today received the money, and he wasted no time getting his promised gift to us. Of this sum, $500 is to be used for the orphanage and the remainder for Mr. Craik's and my own personal expenses.

TALK ABOUT THIS

1. Does it mean "smooth sailing" if we live a life filled with prayers and answers?

2. "The Lord was saying by this poverty, 'I will now see whether you truly lean upon Me and whether you truly look to Me.'" Why do you think God would want to test Mueller like this? Wasn't this already settled by now?

3. If God did the same to you (tested you), what would that look like?

4. In the section, "He Is Always Faithful," are you surprised to read Mueller's answer to the question "what would happen if we ever really did run out of funds, food, or supplies for the children?" Discuss.

5. "How awful would be the disgrace brought upon His Holy Name if we, who have so publicly made our claims that He is always faithful, should in the end bring disgrace to Him, either by unbelief in the hour of trial or by a life of sin in the end." Have you ever thought about your unbelief bringing disgrace to God? If this is true, do you need to repent?

6. What is the difference between "trusting in the Lord" and "trusting in people?" What does it look like?

7. If a stranger examined how you and I lived life (for the past six months), would they come to the conclusion that God must be true? What evidence would they find? Discuss and share.

Application: What if I...?

1. What if I were in a state of "perpetual poverty" with "great needs" and still had faith that God would provide?

2. What if I resolved not to act until I first considered what would most glorify God?

3. What if I really understood that God was the source of everything good I had?

Chapter 4

MUELLER TALKS TO US.
WHAT'S THE DIFFERENCE
BETWEEN MUELLER AND ME?

I WANT EVERY PERSON who reads my journals and stories about the orphanages to have simple confidence in God for everything you need, no matter what your circumstances. I want the answers to prayer you read about here to encourage you to pray more. I want you to pray for the conversion of your friends and family. I want you to pray for your own growth in grace and knowledge, for your Christian friends to stretch their faith and grow, for believers everywhere, and for the success of preaching the gospel.

I especially warn you, Reader, against being led away by the craftiness of Satan, to think that these blessings of living the faith-life are only meant for me and not intended for all children of God. While it is true that every believer is not called by God to establish and run an orphanage, still all believers—including you—are indeed called upon to cast all your burdens on Him and trust in Him for everything. You are not only expected to pray about everything but to expect answers to prayers that are prayed according to His will and in the name of the Lord Jesus.

Do not make the mistake of thinking that I have some rare gift of faith (as mentioned in 1 Corinthians 12:9), and that's why I'm able to trust in the Lord. It is true that the faith I exercise is altogether God's own gift. It's true that He alone supports it, and He alone can increase it. It's also true that moment-by-moment I depend on Him for it and that if I were left to myself for just one moment, my faith would utterly fail.

But it is *not* true that my faith is the gift of faith mentioned in 1 Corinthians 12:9. I say this for the following reasons:

1. Faith is also mentioned in 1 Corinthians 13:2: "If I have a faith that can move mountains, but have not love, I am nothing." This verse seems to refer to the faith mentioned in 1 Corinthians 12:9. This is *not* the faith I exercise to meet my needs and the needs of the orphans. Rather, my faith is the same faith every believer has. This is faith that begins at conversion and grows little by little. Mine is still growing after sixty-nine years.

2. The faith I rely on to provide for my needs is not something that starts small and grows through the years. It is present in the same measure from the beginning.

Take note: For these sixty-nine years, I have never been permitted to doubt that my sins are forgiven, that I am a child of God, and that I shall finally spend eternity with Christ. The reason I do not doubt these things is because God's grace enables me to exercise faith that is based upon the Word of God. God tells me these things in the Bible, and I just believe them.

There are times when, if I were only looking at my situation from the surface, everything would appear to be dark—exceedingly dark. These are the times when I surely would have been overwhelmed with grief and despair. However, at such times I sought God—I grabbed onto faith in His mighty power, His unchangeable love, and His infinite wisdom. When I considered these things, I soon came to realize that God is indeed able and willing to deliver me, if it is for my *good!*

The Bible says, "He who did not spare his own Son, but

gave him up for us all—how will he not also, along with him, graciously give us all things?" (Rom. 8:32). This, then, is what kept me in peace, and this is available to every believer. There is nothing I have done that you cannot do. I have no more access to faith than you do.

In addition, when we had greater trials than just a shortage of funds, I leaned on God even more. For example, when lies were spread around that the orphans didn't have enough food to eat or the children were being abused, it weighed heavily on my heart, and I leaned hard on God.

Sometimes these trials would occur when I was a thousand miles away from home. Occasionally I would be away for several weeks. During these times my soul was fixed on God. I believed His words and knew that His promises were sure. I often fell to my knees before God and poured out my soul. When I arose, I was in peace because the trouble that was stirring in my soul had been cast upon God; it no longer was in me. Thus I was kept in peace even when God's will had taken me a thousand miles away.

When I needed houses, caretakers, staff, or teachers, I simply looked to the Lord for every need and trusted in Him to help.

Dear Reader, it may seem that I am boasting, but by the grace of God, I am not. From the depths of my soul I give God all the credit for what He has enabled me to do. It is God who has enabled me to trust in Him. He has never, ever let me down. My trust in God has never been in vain.

I thought it was important to make these remarks. I didn't want anyone to make the mistake of thinking that my depending on God was a unique, one-time gift from God for me alone, and therefore, not intended for anyone else. Likewise, I don't want anyone to mistakenly think that this faith-based project had only to do with an "easy" way to get money! By the grace of God, it is my heartfelt desire to depend on God for *every* need, from the smallest to the largest of earthly and spiritual concerns of my family, other believers, and the church around the world, as well as for all of the needs of the Bible school.

Dear Reader, do not think I have reached the goal! I am very aware that my own faith-walk must still stretch and grow to reach God's goal for me. I thank God for the faith He has given me. I ask Him to uphold and increase it.

And lastly, once again let me remind you: do not let Satan deceive you into thinking that you cannot have this same faith. If that's what you think, please recognize it for what it is—a lie from Satan.

Here's what I do:

1. When I lose something like a key, I ask the Lord to direct me to it, and I *expect an answer.*

2. When a person with whom I have made an appointment does not show up on time and I begin to be annoyed and worried about getting off schedule, I ask God to hasten him to me, and I *expect an answer.*

3. When I do not understand a passage of scripture, I lift up my heart to the Lord, and ask that His Holy Spirit instruct me; and I *expect to be taught,* though I do not set a deadline for it to be done.

4. When I am preparing to preach, I seek help from the Lord. I know that preaching is not my natural ability, and I am aware how unworthy I am to speak for God; nevertheless, I am not discouraged. Instead, I begin the task cheerfully because I *look for His assistance* and *believe that He will help* me, for the sake of His Son.

5. And that's how I pray! I pray and then I *expect an answer.*

If you are also a believer, don't you think you could do the same? Please don't make the mistake of thinking I am somehow different from you or that I have some extraordinary privileges that other believers do not have. It's just not so!

Try it! Stand still, pray, look for the answer, and if you *trust in Him*, you will see the answer.

Any believer can—and should—do this. But sadly, what I see in the hour of trial, when a believer should be drawing closer than ever to God's heart, instead I see believers forsaking the ways of the Lord. When this happens, the *food of faith*—the very means whereby our faith might be fed and nourished, is lost.

> Every good and perfect gift is from above, coming down from the Father of the heavenly lights, who does not change like shifting shadows.
>
> —JAMES 1:17

This leads me to the following important point. You may ask: how may I, a true believer, have my faith strengthened? Here's how:

1. Notice that the increase of faith is a gift, so it must come from God, and therefore, we should ask Him for this blessing. *Ask God to increase your faith.* Expect an answer.

2. To strengthen your faith you must take time for *careful reading and meditation of the Word.* Through reading the Bible, and especially through meditation on what you're reading, you will become more and more acquainted with the nature and character of God, and thus see more and more besides His holiness and justice—what a kind, loving, gracious, merciful, mighty, wise, and faithful God He is. Therefore, when you are

weighed down by financial stress, physical illness, pain, grief over the death of a beloved family member, or in need of a job, you will find yourself at peace because you have spent regular time reading and meditating on God's own words. You will have learned from Him that God has no limits; there are no limits to His ability to help you. You will know that God has mighty power and infinite wisdom, and you will also read repeatedly of the instances in which His mighty power and infinite wisdom have actually been used in helping and delivering His people. And so you will know that He is likewise willing to help you! Your reading of the Scriptures proves it all to you; you can't miss it. So if God has become known to you through reading, meditation, and prayer, you will become more and more sure of Him. Your doubting habits will gradually fade away.

3. It is incredibly important that you *maintain an upright heart and a clear conscience.* Do not knowingly and habitually behave in ways that you know are sinful. You cannot grow in faith if you do. How could I possibly expect to grow in faith if I habitually grieve Him and seek to detract from God's glory and honor? How can my faith grow if I say I trust and depend on God but then I make choices that are clearly not pleasing to Him? All my confidence in God, all my leaning upon Him in the hour of need will be gone—just like that!— if I have a guilty conscience and make no effort to stop my own sinful behavior. And if I cannot trust in God because of my guilty conscience, then my faith is weakened by that distrust. Here's how it works: with every new trial, my faith either

increases or decreases. If I trust God and God answers my faith-filled prayer, my faith increases.
If I distrust God and live in ways that displease
Him, my faith shrinks every time I choose not to
trust Him. I then have less and less power to look
simply and directly to Him. A habit of self-de-
pendence is created and encouraged. Every single
prayer sends my faith either up or down. Either I
trust in God (in which case I am not trusting in
myself, in others, or in circumstances), or I trust
in myself, others, and/or circumstances (in which
case I am *not* trusting in God). It's one way or the
other, and I make the choice every time I pray.

4. If we're serious about wanting to strengthen our
faith, *we should not shrink from opportunities
where our faith may be tried;* that's how it gets
strengthened! In our natural state, we dislike
dealing with God and God alone. Our natural
alienation from God causes us to shrink from
Him, and this old habit is hard to break even
after we come to faith in Christ. It's a habit that
keeps us from the very place we ought to seek if
we want our faith to be strengthened. Memorize
this position: stand with God and God alone; depend upon Him alone; look to Him alone. The
more opportunities I find to have my faith tried
(regarding my body, my family, my service for the
Lord, my business, etc.), the more opportunities
I have to see God's help and answers to prayer.
Every new situation in which He helps and delivers me will increase my faith. That's why you
should not avoid circumstances in which your
faith may be tried. Instead of cringing, cheerfully embrace each one as an opportunity to see

the hand of God stretched out on your behalf to help and deliver you, and watch how your faith is strengthened.

5. The last important point for the strengthening of your faith is this: *let God work!* When the hour of trial comes, do not maneuver or manipulate a solution of your own. Let Him do it! When God gives faith, it is given (among other reasons) for the very purpose of being tried.

Remember this: however weak your faith may be, God will try it, but He does it gently, gradually, patiently. At first your faith may be tried very little compared to a seasoned, mature believer because God never gives us more than we can bear. But He also provides the faith we need for each trial. When the moment of trial comes, our natural inclination is to distrust God and instead trust in ourselves, in friends, or in circumstances.

It seems easier for us to work it out by ourselves than simply to trust God to act. But if we do not learn to patiently wait for God's help, if we keep working out our own deliverance, then at the next trial of our faith it will be *even harder* to trust Him. We will continue in the downward cycle of not trusting God, choosing instead to work out our own solutions.

However, if we stand still and watch for God's action, see His hand stretched out on our behalf, and trust in Him alone, then our faith will be increased each time. We'll be on an upward cycle that never ends!

If you choose the upward cycle and want to have your faith strengthened, you must remember to *give God time.* This waiting on God to act is how we learn how faithful God is. No shortcuts here. God proves to His child how willing He is to help and deliver, but first God must see that you are willing to wait on Him. The very instant it is good for you, God will act.

TALK ABOUT THIS

1. Do you think Mueller had a "special" calling or unique gift of faith?

2. Where does he get all his faith?

3. What does Mueller do when everything looks "exceedingly dark?"

4. When Mueller has a need, what does he do? How exactly does he pray?

5. When we pray, do we expect an answer?

6. Mueller's observation was that when times are tough, believers usually abandon faith. Is this your observation? Why do you think this happens?

7. "Your reading of the scriptures proves it all to you: you can't miss it." If this statement is true why do you think we "miss it" so often?

8. What five things does Mueller tell us to do in order to strengthen our faith? Which one is hardest for you?

APPLICATION: WHAT IF I...?

1. What if I brought my needs to God and then expected Him to answer?

2. What if I spent more time reading the Bible when I have a difficult situation?

3. What if I embraced the next trial of my faith? Instead of trying to run away from it, what if I faced it straight on and welcomed it as an opportunity to strengthen my faith?

Chapter 5

GETTING TO KNOW
HOW GOD DOES IT
Hint: It's Not the Way We Do It.

Aᴜɢᴜsᴛ 20, 1838: The $25 I received on the eighteenth had been used for housekeeping, so today I was again penniless, but my eyes were lifted up to the Lord. I devoted myself to prayer this morning, knowing I still needed at least $65 more this week, and maybe as much as $100. In answer to prayer, today I received $60 from a lady from Clifton whom I had never met.

Adorable Lord, thank you for this fresh encouragement!

September 10, 1838: Monday morning. No money came in Saturday or Sunday, and it seems that I should draw others in for intensive prayer together. I went to the orphanage and called the staff together. Until now I had never told them about the state of the funds. I now told them about the situation—how much money was needed immediately—and then clearly told them that through all this trial of faith, I still believed that God would provide. I was telling them only because I wanted them to join in the prayer.

I also needed the staff to know that nothing should be purchased that was not needed right now, but they should not hesitate to purchase anything that was necessary for the children. I was clear that the children's needs would not be lacking. Their food and clothing should be provided. I would rather send the children away than have them lacking in basic necessities.

While at the orphanage I also wanted to see if there were any items not being used, thinking I might sell them for cash. The shortage of funds was approaching crisis level.

About 9:30, a quarter came in. Someone had dropped it anonymously into the box at Gideon Chapel. This small amount seemed to me like a promise from God, and I felt assured that He was about to send more.

About 10 o'clock, after I returned from visiting Mr. Craik and praying earnestly with him, a friend stopped by to see my wife and gave her $10 for the orphans. This friend stated that her spirit was greatly stirred, and she felt compelled to come immediately to deliver this money. She also felt that she had already delayed too long.

A few minutes later as I joined my wife, she gave me an additional $10. All this happened without either of them knowing anything at all about our urgent need. Thus I saw again how the Lord encourages my faith.

Right after this, the infants' orphanage called to report some urgent needs, and with these gifts now in hand, I was pleased to provide the needed funds.

September 17, 1838—one week later: The trial still continues. It is now more and more severe with each passing day. Truly I know the Lord has wise purposes in allowing such delays in providing for our needs, and we continue to call on Him for help. I have no doubts that God will send help; we only have to wait on Him.

One of the workers had a little unexpected money come in and he gave us $4; another worker gave us $3, this being all the money she had. With the little funds we had, we were thus able to pay for the needs of the moment and to purchase provisions. Again I rejoice that nothing yet has been lacking in any way!

This evening I felt tired of the long waiting for major funds to arrive, so I went to the Scriptures for some comfort. My soul was greatly refreshed and my faith was strengthened by Psalm 34. I went cheerfully to meet with some of the staff for prayer and read the Psalm to them so they could share in my joy.

September 18, 1838—one day later: Mr. Terry had $6 in hand and I had $1. This $7 enabled us to buy the meat and bread we needed, a little tea for one of the houses, and milk for all—it was all we needed. Thus God has provided more than enough for this day—there is bread for two more days!

However, we are now entirely depleted of funds. Members of the staff, who often give as they are able, have no money left. Now—*watch* how the Lord provides!

A lady from London had arrived four or five days before to visit her daughter and rented a room next door to the boys' orphanage. This afternoon she brought me $15 from her daughter. We were in such dire need that day and that morning that I had asked the Lord if we might be spared from having to sell any items from the homes. The fact that the money had been so near for several days before being given is plain proof that it was always in God's heart to help us, but because He delights in first hearing the prayers of His children, He had allowed us to pray for it first. He also wanted to try our faith, to strengthen it; and He knew the answer would be so much sweeter after the delay.

It is indeed a precious answer. After receiving this money, as soon as I was alone, I burst out into loud praises and thanks!

This evening I met again with the staff for prayer and praise. Everyone's heart was greatly cheered. The money was divided to take care of the needs and will comfortably provide for all that will be needed tomorrow.

July 1, 1845: For the past seven years now, our funds have been consistently nearly exhausted. It has been rare to have more than three days' food and supplies on hand for the one hundred people we support. And yet, in spite of this, only once was my spirit tried. On September 18, 1838, for the first time the Lord seemed not to hear our prayer. But when He did send help, I could see that it was timed perfectly because we were reminded of how truly faithful He is, and so my soul was greatly strengthened and encouraged.

Since that time, I never again distrusted the Lord, even when our immediate situation was *critical*. We have been in deepest poverty some days, and yet I haven't even worried!

Complaints from Neighbors— What Is God Telling Us?

In October 1845, we received a complaint from someone on Wilson Street. Apparently, some of the neighbors do not like having the orphanages on their street. I understood the reasons. Children need space to make noise and play; neighbors like their quiet. After much prayer and meditation, we ended up believing that we should ask the Lord for the means to build a building elsewhere that would accommodate three hundred children.

January 31, 1846: It is now eighty-nine days since we began praying daily about building a new orphanage. It seems to me that the time is near when the Lord will give us a piece of land, and today I told this to the staff after our usual Saturday evening prayer meeting.

February 1, 1846—one day later: A poor widow sent us a gift of $3.

February 2, 1846—one day later: Today I learned about a piece of land on Ashley Down that would be suitable and is available for a very reasonable price.

February 3, 1846—one day later: Saw the land today. It is definitely the most desirable land I have seen. And today someone put an anonymous gift of $1 in the drop box at my house.

February 4, 1846—one day later: This evening I stopped in to see the owner of the land on Ashley Down, but he was not at home. I was told I might find him at his office, so I headed there. When I arrived at his office, they told me I had just missed him; he had been gone only a minute or two. I then considered going back to his home because his staff had told me he would definitely be home no later than 8 o'clock. However, by then it seemed to me that God was putting up a *stop sign*, and I should heed the stop sign and let it rest for today.

February 5, 1846—one day later: This morning I was finally able to meet with the owner of the land we wanted to buy. He told me the most amazing story. He woke up at 3:00 a.m. and couldn't get back to sleep for two hours. During this time, he couldn't get his mind off the land. He knew of my interest, and that I wanted to build an orphanage on the land. As he tossed and turned, he finally decided that if I did approach him about it, he would not only let me have it, but he would reduce the price by 40 percent!

How good is our God!

The agreement was reached this very morning, and I purchased the land (nearly seven acres) at the agreed-upon discounted price.

Notice the way God's hand held me back from finding the owner at home last evening! The Lord wanted to speak to him first during a sleepless night, and bring him to a good decision *before* I was to see him.

Because of His Persistence

November 19, 1846: I am now ready to begin construction, so I am asking the Lord to send me everything needed. Because it is so clear that some of our current neighbors do not like being inconvenienced by the orphanage, I greatly long to be able to move the children from that location as soon as possible. Also, I am becoming more and more convinced that the new location will be much better for the children, both physically and morally. I am also distressed to have a waiting list of applications and not have the space to be able to take the children in. We have a lot of very poor and destitute orphans who need our care.

By God's grace, however, I do not wish to begin construction *one single day* before He wills it. I firmly believe that He will give me every penny needed, *in His own time.* Yet I also know that He delights in being sought after, and that He takes pleasure in hearing our earnest prayers.

For these reasons I gave myself to prayer last evening. I asked that God would send us the means to build the new building. I also prayed for our daily needs; we had received very little since the twenty-ninth of last month.

This morning I prayed again between 5 and 6 o'clock for the building fund, and then enjoyed a long period of Bible reading. I came to Mark 11:24, "Therefore I tell you, whatever you ask for in prayer, believe that you have received it, and it will be yours." I have often felt the impact of this verse and speak of it often, but this morning I felt God's hand press it into my very heart. I applied its truth to our new orphanage; so I said to the Lord, *Lord, I believe you will give me everything I need for this work. I am sure that every need shall be met because I believe that I receive an answer to my prayer.*

And so, with my heart full of peace concerning this building project, I went on to read the rest of the chapter and to the next chapter after that. After family prayer, I returned again to private prayer, as this was now my usual hour for prayer. I prayed for all the many parts of the work, asking God to supply our various needs; and then I asked God to bless every worker who was part of this great work. I asked for blessings on the distribution of Bibles and tracts, on the precious souls in the adult Bible school, on the children's Sunday school, on the six-day schools, and on the four orphanages. And then I prayed again for the means to build the new building.

After this season of prayer, note what happened: In just

five minutes, a registered letter arrived containing a check for $1,500, of which $1,400 is for the building fund! May God's holy name be praised! He is always faithful; the building fund is now at $30,000.

TALK ABOUT THIS

1. Mueller writes about someone giving a quarter. What is his response to this tiny donation? Why do you think he has this view?

2. The title of this chapter is "Getting to Know How God Does It." Defining *it* as the way we manage our lives and provide for our needs, how *does* God do it? Point to some examples. How is this different from the way we do it?

3. How important is timing to God?

4. What did Mueller do when he felt tired of waiting? Did it help?

5. If/when we encounter difficulties, what do we do? How does this contrast with Mueller's approach?

6. Why did Mueller sense God was putting up a "stop sign" on February 4, 1846, as he was trying to purchase land? Does God put up stop signs today?

7. Mueller tells of his own strong desires (he wants to begin building ASAP). Does he view this as a sign to push forward? What does he do and why?

APPLICATION: WHAT IF I...?

1. What if I viewed my own hard times as trials from God?

2. What if I never made a major decision or took action without first spending significant time in Bible reading and heartfelt prayer?

3. What if I stopped being so frustrated when things did not happen as quickly as I planned and instead prayerfully asked God if this might be His doing?

Chapter 6

Buildings, Buildings— You Mean We Need More Than One?

The First One

J ANUARY 25, 1847: The season for building is fast approaching, and therefore, I have begun praying with increased earnestness. I am pleading with the Lord to send the remainder of funds needed. Lately I am sensing that the time is almost here when we will indeed have all the funds needed.

During my prayers, I am again reminding God of all the reasons for building this new building. It is now fourteen months and three weeks since I began praying for this project, and I have been faithful to do so every single day.

This morning I rose from my knees in full confidence, knowing that God not only *could*, but that He *would* send the means, and that it would be soon. Not once in all these fourteen months and three weeks have I had the least doubt that I would have every single need met.

So now, dear Reader, rejoice and praise God with me. About an hour after I prayed, a man gave me $10,000 for the building fund, bringing the total received to $46,425. I cannot describe the joy I felt in God when I received this donation! You cannot know unless you experience it yourself. I have waited upon God for 447 days, praying faithfully; and today I am filled with joy to serve such an amazing God!

How great is the blessing the soul receives by trusting in

God and by waiting patiently. Is it not clear how precious it is to carry on God's work in this way, even when it comes to money? The new total for the building fund is $78,920.

Second and Third Orphanages

March 12, 1862: In November 1850 I began to think about enlarging our capacity from three hundred children to one thousand or more. I began praying daily about this but kept it secret until June 1851 when I began to talk with others about it. From November 1850 to this day, not a single day has gone by without bringing this to the Father in prayer, and generally it has been more than once a day.

But only now, on this day, has this prayer been answered fully. Today we are opening the third orphanage!

I wish to point out to the reader how much time passed before this prayer was finally and fully answered. Sometimes thousands or tens of thousands of prayers are prayed before being answered. This is true even if those prayers are believing prayers, earnest prayers, prayers that are offered in the name of the Lord Jesus, and even though we may be asking purely for the sake of the Lord's honor. This is my testimony: by the grace of God, I continued this prayer every day for more than eleven years, praying without any doubting at all. I never wavered. I continued to seek only the glory of God in all of this.

Praying Three Times a Day for Helpers

For the expanded needs of this new orphanage, I have also prayed daily that God would send me the staff needed for the various departments. Before a single stone was laid, I began to pray for the workers. And as the building progressed, I continued day by day to bring this matter before God, feeling assured that, as in everything else, in this also He would graciously provide for our need for workers. God knew that the whole work was intended for His honor and glory.

Finally the day was near when the orphanage would be opened, and therefore, it was time to review the stack of employment applications that had come in during the past two years. To our surprise, we now discovered that while we had about fifty applications on hand, some positions could not be filled, either because the applicants had married and were no longer available, or upon careful review, some were found unsuitable.

This realization hit us hard. I wondered why this was the case. After all, I had prayed faithfully, day by day, for many years now for this specific, particular need. The need for good, qualified staff had been provided for the second orphanage; why not for this one? I had prayed earnestly; I had expected help; I was so confident; and yet now when the time came, we were lacking.

What now? Reader, what should we do now?

Should we conclude that God was unfaithful? Have we now learned that it is a mistake to trust Him? Are confident prayers useless?

Absolutely not!

On the contrary, this is what I did: I thanked God for all the help He had already given me throughout this project. I thanked Him for enabling me to overcome so many great difficulties. And I thanked Him for the helpers He had provided for the second orphanage. I also thanked Him for the wonderful helpers He had already provided for this new orphanage.

And then, instead of now distrusting God, I looked at this delay as only a *trial of faith*; and therefore resolved that instead of praying *once* a day with my dear wife for this need (as we had been doing daily for years), we would meet *three times* a day to bring this before God. I also brought the need before the entire staff and requested their prayers as well.

Thus I have now continued for four more months in prayer, day by day calling upon God three times each day for this need. The result has been that one helper after another has been provided. Not one person arrived too late. Not one time was the work thrown into confusion. Never once were we delayed in taking in children. And so I am fully assured that the few who are still needed will also be found, when they are *really* needed.

FOURTH AND FIFTH ORPHANAGES

Since May 26, 1864, I have received more than $135,000 for the building fund. I continued to wait patiently for God's timing, being determined to do nothing until I had at least half of the money needed for the two new buildings. We are now $2,000 over the halfway mark; and after again seeking counsel from God, I am ready to take steps toward the purchase of land.

For several years I have had my eye on a beautiful piece of land that seems perfect for our needs. It is conveniently located near the main highway and nearly adjacent to our third orphanage. It is about eighteen acres, with a small house on one end. I have prayed over this piece of land hundreds of times. I prayed that God would find me worthy to be allowed to build two more orphanages on this land. As I stopped and gazed at it, the glistening dew drops looked to me like sparkling jewels of prayer that covered the whole land. It just *looked* like God's land.

I could have bought it years ago, but that would have been going ahead of God. Indeed, I had the money in hand to pay for it years ago, but it was far more important to me to wait on God's timing. I waited patiently, submissively, for God to mark it clearly and distinctly and show that His time had come. If I ran out ahead of God's timing and direction and proceeded to do my own work and not the Lord's, I knew clearly that I could not expect God's blessing.

But now the time had arrived. The Lord was clearly and distinctly leading; and after again going before God in prayer for guidance and being assured that it was indeed His will, I moved forward. I had enough money in hand to pay for the land and to build one house.

The first thing I did was find the agent who represented the owner. I asked him whether the land was for sale. He replied that it was indeed for sale, but it was leased until March 25, 1867. He did not know the price and agreed to write to the owner to find out.

Here was a great difficulty. We wanted to purchase and begin building immediately, and this lease was not up for another two years and four months. However, I was not discouraged at this news. I expected that through prayer, we would negotiate a satisfactory arrangement with the tenant. I planned to make him a fair offer to buy him out of his lease. However, before I had time to do this, two other greater difficulties presented themselves: (1) The owner was asking $35,000 for the land, which was considerably more than it was worth; and (2) I learned that Bristol Waterworks Company intended to construct an additional reservoir for their water on this very land, and they were getting an Act of Parliament passed to make it happen.

Now think about this. Notice how the Lord has brought me this far. He has provided me with the funds needed; following thousands of prayers, He was now directing me to move forward; and there were hundreds of children needing a home. And yet, after God Himself had done all this, it looked as though He was allowing this apparent death-blow to come upon the entire project.

But I have seen God work in this way literally hundreds of times since I first came to know and follow Him. The difficulties that He allows to come are only allowed *for our benefit*! God knows we need to exercise our faith and patience...and more prayer, and more patience. When we exercise our faith God will remove the barriers.

Now because I knew the Lord, these difficulties were not a

big deal to me at all. I knew what to do. I put my trust in Him, according to God's own words:

> The LORD is a refuge for the oppressed, a strong-
> hold in times of trouble. Those who know your
> name will trust in you, for you, LORD, have never
> forsaken those who seek you.
>
> —PSALM 9:9–10

It was time for earnest prayer concerning all these problems. I prayed several times daily about this, and took the following action:

I spoke with the Acting Committee of the directors of the Bristol Waterworks Company regarding their intended reservoir on the land and inquired about their intentions. They courteously told me they would only need a small portion of the land, not enough to interfere with my purpose, and that if they could not find a way to construct their reservoir without interfering with my proposed orphanage, then they would not proceed.

After a lot of prayer, I then proceeded to meet with the current tenant. I was adamant that, as Christians, we would treat him well. At our meeting I told him about my plans to build an orphanage and proposed a settlement with him that would take care of his needs. He said that he would consider the matter and asked for a few days to think it over. A week later I saw him again. He kindly stated that since the land was for such a noble purpose, he would not stand in the way. He had, however, paid a good deal for his lease, and expected compensation for terminating early, which I had already intended to do. This, then, was the second answer to prayer.

Now it was time to deal with the third and most difficult negotiation—the price of the land. It was clear how much the land was worth to the orphanages, but its value to us was not the market value. Therefore, I gave myself to focused prayer for several days, asking that God would compel the owner to accept my offer, which was considerably lower than his asking price. To substantiate my offer, I also pointed out to him why it was not worth what he was asking. He finally agreed to take $27,500 (far less than his asking price of $35,000), and we had our agreement.

The land had several important features: it was fairly level, saving us money before even beginning construction; there was a new sewer running near the field; and there was a gas line accessible nearby. Lastly, and most important of all, this new land was very close to the other three houses already in operation, so all could easily be under the direction of one superintendent. In fact, no other piece of land, near or far, would give us so much advantage.

The Lord has been good to us!

Now that everything has been settled, I proceeded to have the land conveyed to the same trustees who were serving the other three orphanages.

I have elaborated on these details for the sake of the readers. None of you should be discouraged by difficulties, however great, however many, however varied. Give yourself to prayer! Trust God! Expect Him to help. In His own time, and in His own way, He surely will.

March 5, 1874: The fourth and fifth orphanages have now been in operation for several years. More than 1,200 orphans have been cared for here, and we continue to take in more as some of them reach adulthood and move on with good jobs. I delight to note that all expenses were met in full—both for the construction of the new buildings and all necessary furnishings. We even had an excess balance of $20,000 and have used that to keep the houses in good repair.

Please note, dear Reader, how abundantly God answered our prayers and how plain it is that we were not at all mistaken in this. This is because we patiently and prayerfully took the time to determine what His will was. So—be encouraged! Take all your concerns to the living God!

Talk About This

1. Are you surprised that Mueller prayed every single day for more than eleven years regarding the expansion to three orphanages? Would you do that? Why or why not?

2. After years of daily, faithful prayer for staff, what did Mueller do when it looked like the need was not met? How did he view this apparent lack?

3. How important was timing to Mueller?

4. According to Mueller, why does God allow difficulties to come?

5. Mueller says, "These difficulties were not a big deal to me at all." What were the three difficulties? Are they major or minor items? What would you do? Discuss.

6. How does Mueller balance the need for prayer and the need for action?

APPLICATION: WHAT IF I...?

1. What if I took a new look at why God allows difficulties to come to me?

2. What if I viewed my own hard times as trials from God?

3. What if I was faithful to pray every day for things I knew to be God's will?

Chapter 7

MORE ANSWERS TO PRAYER

THE ARTIST'S STORY

APRIL 30, 1859: Today I received the following letter:

Dear Christian brother,

I am the husband of Mrs. Jones, who is sending you the enclosed donation. What could be a better investment than to deposit it in the "Bank of Christ," a bank that always pays the best interest and never fails!

Now, my friend, I am delighted to tell you the following story. I am an artist—a poor artist—a simple landscape painter. About two weeks ago I sent a painting to Bristol for exhibition, just as I finished the book you loaned me. I prayed earnestly that God would find a buyer for my painting, and decided that if it sold, I would send you half the proceeds. The painting was priced at $100.

I can hardly believe what happened! Immediately after the exhibition opened, God in His mercy, having heard my prayer, sent a buyer! Now, I have placed my paintings in Bristol many times before, but have never sold a single painting!

My heart is still leaping for joy! I have never been so near to God. Through your life, I have learned to draw closer to God, to trust Him more, and to exercise more faith than ever before. The sale of this painting is the first I have sold in the past twelve months! What a blessing God has given me! What joy as I read your book! And now, my painting is on display in the academy of arts at Clifton and included in their catalogue.

I have had thousands of such letters over the past forty years, and each one touches my soul.

BOLD PRAYER: IS GOD IN CHARGE OF THE WIND?

Toward the end of November 1857, we had an unexpected breakdown of the furnace at building number one. We knew it was impossible to get through the winter without repairs. To know that and not do anything about replacing it—to simply say that I will trust God regarding it—would be careless presumption, not faith in God. It would be counterfeit faith.

The furnace was boxed in with brickwork. We couldn't even assess the situation without tearing down bricks. And yet here we are, right at the onset of the winter season with a defective furnace. What were we to do? We had not expected this. I was keenly aware that we had three hundred children and infants who needed to be kept warm.

To purchase and install a new furnace would take weeks, and the weather was already growing cold. Repairing the old one was questionable, and then there was the issue of having to tear down bricks just to assess the damaged unit. Even doing that would take days. How were we to keep three hundred children warm in the meantime?

I considered bringing in some portable gas stoves, but we learned that these small stoves would be unable to heat the large rooms, plus each one would require a chimney to vent the carbon monoxide outdoors. The small stoves would only work for small rooms or hallways anyway.

Someone suggested the temporary installation of Arnott's stoves, but these were also unsuitable and required venting. I was growing increasingly concerned and knew we needed to find a solution soon.

Finally I knew that I must throw myself entirely into the hands of God, knowing that He is merciful and compassionate. After prayer, I decided to open the brick chamber to see what the extent of the damage was and determine if there was any hope of repairing it, at least enough to get us through the winter.

The day was scheduled for the workmen to come. We knew we would have to allow the fire to go completely out so repairs could be done.

But notice what happened next! A frigid north wind started to blow on the Thursday before the scheduled Wednesday repairs. Now we had our first really cold weather, which raised the question, how in the world could we allow the fire to go out with weather this bitter cold? It was just not possible with three hundred small children and infants here. And yet, we knew without doing something, the furnace would probably just quit at some point.

What were we supposed to do? The repairs could not be delayed. And so I asked the Lord for two things: (1) that He would please change that bitter north wind into a warm south wind, and (2) that He would cause the workmen to work with all their heart and accomplish their work quickly. I remembered how much Nehemiah accomplished in just fifty-two days while building the walls of Jerusalem because the people "worked with all their heart."

Well, the fateful Wednesday arrived. That Tuesday evening the bitter north wind was still blowing, but Wednesday morning it changed into a warm south wind—exactly as I had prayed! The weather became so mild that no fire was needed at all. The brickwork was removed, the leak was found very quickly, and the workmen applied themselves diligently to their task. Toward the end of the day, their supervisor arrived to check on their progress. He informed us that they would work late tonight and return very early the next morning.

Upon hearing this, the foreman said, "Sir, we would rather work all night and finish the work." When I heard this, I remembered my second prayer—that God would cause them to "work with all their heart."

And so it was, by morning the repair was completed. The leak was repaired (even though with great difficulty), and within about thirty hours the brickwork was restored, and the fire was hot again; all while the warm south wind blew.

Here, then, is another story of how God took care of our daily needs as we were faithful in prayer.

CONVERSION OF THE CHILDREN

May 26, 1860: Day after day, year after year, by the help of God, we labor in prayer for the spiritual welfare of the orphans. These prayers have continued in earnest for twenty-four years now, and have been abundantly answered. We have seen hundreds of the children commit their lives to Christ. There have been several times when we witnessed the conversion of many of the children within a very short time, sometimes very suddenly.

We had such a season about three years ago when within a few days about sixty children came to faith in the Lord Jesus. This happened twice that year.

In July 1859 the Spirit of God moved so mightily among one of our schools that more than half the children were deeply convicted of their sin and trusted Christ. This proved to be more than a passing excitement or emotion-filled experience. Now a year later, these children continue to follow Christ with confidence. By my count, this amounts to sixty-three out of the one hundred twenty children in that school who came to Christ that July.

This extraordinary work of the Holy Spirit cannot be traced to any particular cause. It was, however, a most precious answer to prayer. This really encourages us to continue to pray for the conversion of the other children.

Another season of seeing the Holy Spirit move powerfully among the children occurred during the end of January and beginning of February 1860. The details are fascinating. It actually began among the younger children—little girls from six to nine years old. It then spread to the older girls, then to the boys; so that within about ten days more than two hundred of the children were stirred in their souls. We saw them one by one pray and find peace through faith in the Lord Jesus.

They then asked permission to hold their own prayer meetings, and they have had these meetings ever since. Many of them began writing letters to their friends and relatives urging them to also follow Christ.

APPRENTICE JOBS FOR THE BOYS

June 1, 1862: In the early part of summer 1862, we had several boys who were ready for graduation and jobs as apprentices. The problem was we had no applications from master craftsmen to hire them. Virtually all of our boys are eventually sent out as apprentices, so this recruitment and assignment process is a major part of our program. We insist on several criteria: (1) the master craftsmen must be Christians, (2) the nature of the business must be honorable, (3) the position must be suitable for the particular boy, and (4) the master craftsman must be willing to bring the boy into his own family.

With these criteria we brought it all to prayer, as we had done for more than twenty years. As was our practice, we did not advertise at all. We knew how good God had been to us in providing apprentice appointments for our boys for the past twenty years, having placed hundreds in good positions. We also knew this was not easy.

Several weeks passed with nothing. So we continued in prayer. Suddenly one application arrived, and then another; and we now report that eighteen successful placements have been accomplished. We take note that this was done entirely by prayer. Every boy who was ready for placement has been placed.

Danger! Sickness at the Orphanages

October 1, 1866: During the summer and autumn of 1866 we had an outbreak of measles at all three orphanages. When this began, we focused our prayers:

1. We prayed that there might not be too many children sick at any one time so we would be able to care for them in our sick rooms. This prayer was totally answered. Even though lots of children became sick (eighty-three, one hundred eleven, and sixty-eight in three homes), yet God heard our prayer and each time the sick rooms were full, no one else got sick until some recovered and returned to their rooms.

2. We also prayed that each child who got sick with the measles might recover and not die. And thus it was. God graciously answered this prayer. Although 262 got the measles, not one died.

3. We prayed that no children would suffer any lasting physical complications from this disease (as so often happens). This prayer was also granted. All 262 children not only recovered, but did well afterwards.

I am so grateful to God for His mercy and blessing through this trial. He is gracious to answer prayer, to the honor of His name.

TALK ABOUT THIS

1. In The Artist's Story, what three things did the artist learn from watching Mueller's life? What three things would someone learn from watching your life?

2. Mueller writes about an "unexpected breakdown of the furnace." Do you think God allows breakdowns to occur in order to show His glory? Discuss.

3. Notice how specific Mueller was in his prayers (that God would change the wind, and that God would cause the workmen to work diligently). In your experience, is this a common way of praying? Why or why not?

4. Before the scheduled repairs to the furnace, Mueller prayed for two specific things. With three hundred infants and toddlers in his care, what was his "Plan B?"

5. When praying for apprentice placements, "several weeks passed with nothing. So we continued in prayer." Why do you think, after several weeks passed, Mueller didn't give up, or change something?

6. During the measles outbreak, why do you think Mueller did not pray for the miracle of no measles at all?

APPLICATION: WHAT IF I...?

1. What if I asked God for very specific things?

2. What if I viewed "unexpected" occurrences to be the hand of God?

3. What if I never gave up when I prayed for something I knew was God's will?

Chapter 8

PRAYERS, ANSWERS, THEN WHAT? JOY!

DECEMBER 27, 1863: The end of the year was upon us, and in closing the books I really wanted to send financial support to other missionaries. So I went through my list of names, marking the ones I had not previously sent any money to and writing down the amount I wanted to send to each one. The list totaled $2,380, but all I had on hand was $1,400. I wrote a check for $1,400, though I would gladly have sent $2,380, but was thankful that I was able to send at least this much.

Having written this check as my last task for the day, I then turned to my usual season of prayer for the many things that I brought to the Lord daily. Today I added to my prayers the needs of these faithful missionaries, and asked God to even now provide me with the means to send more before the end of the year, which was now just three days away.

I then went home about 9 o'clock and found that a donation had arrived. Five hundred dollars was designated for missionary support, $500 was at my disposal, and $25 was for my personal needs. Therefore, I took the whole $1,000 for missions and thus had enough to cover the rest of the list I had made previously.

Anyone who knows the blessings of really trusting in God and seeing how He sends help in direct response to specific prayer will know the incredible joy I had when I sent this donation. It was both the answer to prayer and the provision for many devoted servants of Christ.

September 30, 1869: The joy that comes from seeing God answer our prayers cannot be described! We get momentum that is so great, and it drives us further forward. I wish all my Christian readers could experience this great happiness. If you truly trust Christ for your salvation, if you walk uprightly and do not harbor sin in your heart, if you continue to wait patiently and believingly in God, then you will surely receive answers to your prayers!

You may not be called upon to serve God the way I am, and therefore, never have the exact type of experiences I have with prayer, but in your own unique life—your family, your business, your profession, your church position, your work for the Lord, etc., you may indeed have answers just as distinct as anything I have recorded here.

THE GREATEST NEED OF ALL

However, if this is ever read by anyone who is not a believer in the Lord Jesus, someone who is drifting along in carelessness or the self-righteousness of their unrepentant hearts, then I want to lovingly plead with you first of all to be reconciled to God by putting your trust in the Lord Jesus. You are a sinner. You deserve punishment for your sin. If you can't see this, ask God to show it to you. Let this be your very first prayer.

After God shows you how sinful your nature is, then ask Him to show you the Lord Jesus. God sent Him; He takes the punishment that you deserve for your sins. In His amazing grace, God accepts the obedience and sufferings of Jesus as payment for your sin and my sin. The very moment you believe in the Lord Jesus, you have forgiveness for all your sins.

When this happens, you are reconciled to God; and you now are invited to boldly approach God and come into His very presence. You can tell Him your requests; and the more you realize that your sins are forgiven, that God for Christ's sake is pleased with all those who believe on Him, the more ready you will be to come and bring all your wants (physical, earthly, and spiritual) to the heavenly Father, asking Him to provide for your needs.

However, if you choose to remain in your sin and not seek God's forgiveness, then you will always be kept at a distance from God, especially regarding prayer. Therefore, dear Reader, if you are still in your sins, let your first prayer be to ask God to reveal Jesus, His beloved Son, to you.

A DOUBLE ANSWER

August 25, 1865: I received the following letter today from London with $500:

> My dear Sir,
>
> I believe God has prompted me to send you this money. I hope that you are doing well.
>
> Yours in Christ,
> John

I have never met this man in person; however, he has sent me large donations several times. Two days before receiving this last donation, I had asked God specifically if He would please prompt this generous man again to send a donation (something I had never done before). And now I receive a double answer to prayer: the donation itself, and the fact that it had come from *this* man—exactly as I had prayed.

Notice what the letter said: "I believe God has prompted me to send you this money." Truly I see now that it was indeed the Lord who nudged this gentleman to send me this check.

As you read this, perhaps you may assume that when I wrote to thank him, that I relayed this story to him. I did not. My reason was I didn't want him to think I was in dire need and thus may have influenced him to send more and that would have violated my primary vow—that I would never appeal to a single person to meet our needs.

In truly knowing the Lord, in really relying on God and God alone, there is no need to drop hints, either directly or indirectly, in order to induce individuals to give. In my thank you note, I might have said that I need a certain amount each day to keep the operations going and that would have been a true statement. I could have also told him that I still needed $100,000 to move forward with our plans to enlarge the orphanages. But my practice is never to allude to any of these things in my correspondence with donors. When we publish our annual reports, everyone who wants to can see how matters stand. And so I leave these things in God's hands. I let God do the speaking to the hearts of His children. And I can't help but noticing God does this very well! We do not wait on God in vain!

CHRISTIANS IN BUSINESS—MUELLER'S ADVICE

About a year ago, a Christian businessman wrote to me seeking advice regarding a difficult business issue. His letter indicated a strong interest in honoring Christ through his business; his desire was to glorify God. His circumstances, however, were putting him in a very difficult position.

I invited him to come to Bristol so we could spend some time together, so he made the long journey to come here. As we spent time together, he told me the details of his situation. He was right; it was indeed very challenging.

I advised him to do the following:

1. Each day he should set aside some specific time with his wife for focused prayer when they could spread their business difficulties before God in prayer. If possible, do this twice a day.

Be on the lookout for answers to these prayers. Expect that God will send help.

2. Avoid any manipulative attempts to attract customers (such as advertising a couple of items below cost). Doing this may result in missing the help God plans to send.

3. Set aside a percentage of profits for God, no matter if the profit is small or large. Be faithful in this.

4. Lastly, I asked him to report back to me, month by month, on how God deals with him through this.

The reader will be interested to know that from this time on, God prospered his business. His profits went up 38 percent over the previous year, which is remarkable. He has made donations to the orphanages and has also been able to support other charitable works.

REVIVAL IN THE ORPHANAGES

In the 1872 annual report, I told about the spiritual revival that had spread through the orphanages; but because this is such an important subject, I want to discuss it more fully here.

Prior to this, the spiritual condition of the children was very poor and caused us a lot of sadness. There were very few children who earnestly loved God and sought to follow Him. Aware of this, we had begun to bring it to the whole staff for prayer. We did this in each of our full-staff meetings and in private prayers as well.

In answer to these prayers, many of the children came to faith in Christ in 1872. The Lord began His work among the children on January 8, 1872, and continued for quite some time. Orphanage number three did not see this revival until God allowed smallpox to sweep heavily through the house. From that time on, we saw the working of the Holy Spirit there as well.

At the end of July 1872, I received reports from all five of the houses reporting that a total of 729 of the children were now believers in the Lord Jesus. This is by far more than we have ever had before! All glory and praise to God!

We see how God overruled the terror of smallpox, and indeed turned it into an incredible blessing! We are thankful that we had this opportunity to go to God in prayer, trust Him, and see these amazing results!

TALK ABOUT THIS

1. Mueller often writes about "incredible joy" he experiences when he sees answers to his prayers. Do you observe this today? Why or why not? According to Mueller, who *does* experience this joy?

2. If you have an experience of a direct answer to a specific prayer with resulting joy, share with the group.

3. Mueller gives three specific conditions that must be met if we are to receive answers to our prayers. What are they? Which one is hardest? Which one is easy to miss? Discuss.

4. Mueller invites unbelievers to trust Christ, and then they can "boldly approach God." Have you seen unbelievers pray for things they wanted? Do unbelievers expect God to do things for them? Discuss.

5. Why do you think Mueller advised the businessman to pray *with* his wife?

6. How important is it to pray with a partner?

7. Why do you think Mueller advises the business-man to "set aside a percentage of his profits for God?" Do you think this is important? Why or why not?

8. Mueller links the smallpox epidemic with the spiritual revival of the children, especially in building number three. Why do you think these two events are related?

APPLICATION: WHAT IF I...?

1. What if I told others when God answered a very specific prayer of mine?

2. What if I told my non-Christian friends about my answers to prayer? Would that open up a conversation so I could lead them to Christ?

3. What if I prayed with my spouse or partner every day?

Chapter 9

MISSIONS!

It's Bigger Than My Little World

Editor's note: In 1875, at the age of seventy, George Mueller began twenty years of missionary tours. These tours took him to forty-two countries, where he preached to more than three million people. He was fluent in several languages and preached without the need for an interpreter.

W E BEGAN OUR ninth missionary tour on August 8, 1882. The first place I preached was Weymouth (England), where I spoke four times. From there we went to Calais (France), Brussels (Belgium), and Dusseldorf on the Rhine (Germany), a place where I had often preached six years ago. This time I preached there eight times. Staying at Dusseldorf was interesting.

During our first visit there (in 1876), a wonderful local missionary came to me one day seeking my advice. He had six sons, none of whom were at all interested in following Christ, though he had prayed for them for many years. I told him to continue praying for them, expect an answer, and praise God.

Now six years later I am again in Dusseldorf and this dear man came to me to report what had happened. "I am surprised I had not figured it out for myself," he said. "After seeking you, I resolved to heed your advice, and I prayed more earnestly than ever." He then reported that two months later five of his six sons committed their lives to Christ (within eight days), and all five continue to walk with Christ to this day. His sixth son was beginning to show interest and he expected that God would soon answer prayer for him.

Christian Reader, be encouraged! If your prayers are not answered all at once, don't stop praying! Instead, wait on God and continue praying even more earnestly, all the while *expecting* answers.

GOD'S PLAN TO SEND OUT FOREIGN MISSIONARIES

Editor's note: The Bristol Church (George Mueller's church) was a great example of how churches can send out missionaries around the world. They did it by prayer. George Mueller writes about this in his journal.

During the eight years before I went to preach in Germany, several of us in the church began to sense the need to pray that God would honor us by calling forth believers to go out and preach in foreign lands. For a long time this prayer seemed to be unanswered.

Now, however, the Lord was about to answer it, and I was to be the first one to go. It was fitting—I was the one who had especially sensed the need, and I was the one who would carry God's truth to others.

About that time the Lord called Mr. and Mrs. Barrington to go to Demerara, South America, and Mr. and Mrs. Espenett to go to Switzerland. Both of these couples left shortly after I left for Germany. But that was not all. On the day these two couples left, Mr. Mordal, who had faithfully served God in our local church for twelve years, was moved to follow in their steps; and so, eleven months later he also departed for missionary service. He and I together had prayed faithfully these past eight years that God would call laborers to go out as missionaries. Of all the people in our church,

Mr. Mordal seemed the least likely candidate to be called, but God called him.

And so he went. He worked for a while in Demerara, and then God called him home.

When we ask God for something, such as laborers for the harvest or that God would provide the means for such work, the honest question must be put to our own hearts: Am *I* willing to go, if He calls me? Am *I* willing to give according to my ability? We may be the very person the Lord calls. We may have the very money God will use to provide for the needs.

> *Editor's note: In the 1896 Annual Report for the Bible school, George Mueller reports how much God honored this local church.*

From our own church, sixty people have gone out to serve as missionaries. Some of them have gone straight from their missionary service to heaven, but there are about forty still working faithfully at their assignments.

Is there any reason why the great needs in Asia, Africa, and all around the world should not be met by the thousands of churches in Europe and America following this divine plan of praying to the Lord of the harvest that He would send forth laborers from among them? Surely believers can expect God to answer their prayers as He answered the prayers of the Bristol Church.

Look what has been done in China by the faithful use of God's method! Missionary Hudson Taylor writes these words in *China's Millions*:

> We followed God's direction to obtain workers. ('Ask the Lord of the harvest, therefore, to send out workers into his harvest field.') This is exactly how we found the very first five workers, before the Mission was even formed.

We did the same to get the next twenty-four workers; the same when further reinforcements were needed; and later for seventy more in three years, and even for one hundred in one year. From time to time, we prayed in further additions as needed, and have relied on this plan for every need.

Is it possible that these results could have been obtained through any other means? God assembled a unique band of workers from nearly every denomination, from many countries. He gathered and kept them together for thirty years with no other bond except that which the call of God and the love of God provided! This band now numbers more than seven hundred men and women, and they are aided by more than five hundred native workers.[1]

AN IRISHMAN LEARNS ABOUT MUELLER (WATCH WHAT HAPPENS NEXT!)

In November 1856, Mr. James McQuilkin, a young Irishman, gave his life to the Lord. Soon after he came across an advertisement for one of my books that contained my early journals about my prayer experiences. The ad greatly interested him, so in January 1857 he bought the book. God used it to bless him, and as he read the book, he saw how God answered believing prayer. He recognized that everything I had done through prayer, he could do also.

And so he determined to begin his own prayer journey. The first thing he prayed for was a spiritual partner—someone who would believe and pray with him. He soon met a young man and the two began praying together. Now that his first prayer was answered, James asked God to lead him to a few more men who would join them for prayer.

The Lord soon gave them two more men, and in the fall of 1857, James told these three men about my book and how reading it had taught him the power of believing prayer. He proposed to the group that they pray together to seek God's blessing upon their various Sunday school work, prayer meetings, and preaching.

In the fall 1857 these four men met for prayer every Friday evening in a little schoolhouse in the town of Connor. By this time a great revival had begun to sweep across the United States, and James began to long for such a revival in Ireland, his beloved home country. He was beginning to realize that all things are possible through simple, believing prayer.

On January 1, 1858, God gave this little group the first remarkable answer to prayer—the conversion of a farmer. He was taken into the group of four, and shortly after that another young man was converted, who also joined the group. These additions greatly encouraged the original four.

God began to send them more. New converts were brought into the group. They read scripture, prayed, and shared thoughts with each other from their individual Bible reading. Even though more and more people were converted, it was all happening quietly, with no outward notice or advertising.

In late December 1858, one of the new converts returned to his hometown, spoke to his old friends about their need for Christ, and told them what was happening in Connor. His friends were interested and wanted to meet some of the Connor group. James McQuilkin and two of the original partners agreed to travel there to preach and tell their stories.

Some believed; some mocked; others thought there was a great deal of presumption in these young converts, yet many wanted to have another meeting. On February 16, 1859, James and his friends held another meeting.

This was the date the Holy Spirit began to work mightily. Many were converted, and from that time on, conversions occurred rapidly. Some of these new converts went to other places and carried the spiritual fire with them. This blessed work of God spread everywhere they went.

On April 5, 1859, James went to Ballymena (a prominent city in Ireland) to hold a meeting in a Presbyterian Church. On April 11 he went to another Presbyterian Church. Several people were convicted of their sin and received Christ and His forgiveness at these meetings.

On May 28, 1859, James and Jeremiah Meneely (one of the original group) went to Belfast to hold a meeting. During the first week James conducted meetings in five different Presbyterian Churches; that was the beginning of the blessed work in Belfast. It seemed that the Holy Spirit just spread like wildfire from this work, for each new convert was used by God to carry the truth from one place to another.

Such was the beginning of that mighty work of the Holy Spirit, and it led to the conversion of hundreds of thousands. Some readers will remember that in 1859 this Holy Spirit fire was spread across Ireland, England, Wales, and Scotland, and how the continent of Europe was swept by this mighty working of God's Holy Spirit. It led thousands to give themselves to the work of preaching. This great movement continued through 1874.

It almost goes without saying that none of this happened because of any person's great talents; it was clearly the work of the Holy Spirit alone. And yet I state these facts so everyone can see what delight God has in answering the believing prayers of His children.

TALK ABOUT THIS

1. If someone asked you for advice regarding their grown children, who had no interest in Christ,

what would you advise? What did Mueller advise? What was the result? Are Mueller's results different than ours? Why?

2. By now we've seen how often Mueller tells people to *expect* answers when they pray. Why do you think is this so important?

3. When you read how much impact the Bristol church had on the world, are you surprised? Why do you think this happened?

4. James McQuilkin "saw how God answered believing prayer." Is there any *real* difference between this and the phrase commonly used today: God answers prayer? Discuss.

5. What was the very first thing McQuilkin prayed for? Why?

6. McQuilkin, an ordinary man, prayed and followed God's leading and eventually saw hundreds of thousands of people converted. Do you think this means he was not really ordinary? What does it mean?

APPLICATION: WHAT IF I...?

1. What if I expected an answer *each* time I prayed?

2. What if I began to pray and seek God's bigger plan for my life?

3. What if I looked for ways to bring delight to God?

Chapter 10

GEORGE MUELLER'S MARRIAGE AND HIS BIGGEST TEST EVER

Editor's note: This is George Mueller's account of how God led him to meet and later marry his wife, Mary.

G OD SHOWED ME clearly that Mary was to be my wife. At the end of 1829 I left London to preach in Devonshire. A fellow believer handed me a note with the name and address of a well-known Christian lady, Miss Paget. He thought I should meet her because she was influential and might be able to help my work.

I put the note in my pocket but promptly forgot about it. Three weeks later I felt God prompting me to call on her. Only later did I realize that God was using this to introduce me to my excellent wife.

Miss Paget asked me to preach in January 1830 in Poltimore, a nearby village where Mr. Groves used to preach before he went to Baghdad to serve as a missionary. I was glad to accept the invitation because my soul has been filled with a longing to tell everyone the truth about the Lord's return and other vitally important truths.

Before I left Miss Paget, she told me where Mr. Groves used to stay and said that I could probably rent a room there when I was in town. I went there to inquire about a room, and that is where I met my beloved Mary. She worked for Mr. and Mrs.

Hake (the homeowners) and was especially helpful in managing the household. I began to preach there once a month and then once a week, each time staying at the boarding house where Mary worked.

Prior to this I had decided not to marry at all, thinking that I would be free to travel and preach; but after several months I began to realize that it would be better for me (a young twenty-four-year-old pastor) to be married. That opened up a perplexing question for me: whom should I marry? Mary Groves was in my thoughts, so I spent a lot of time in prayer first. I was concerned for the Hakes, knowing that they had come to depend on Mary. So I prayed again and again.

Slowly I began to realize that Mary was also growing fond of me, and as this became increasingly obvious, I knew it was time to propose marriage to her. I did not want to leave Mr. Hake in a bad situation, so I prayed that God would give him a suitable helper to replace Mary.

On August 15, 1830, I wrote to Mary, asking her to become my wife; and on August 19 when I arrived for my weekly preaching, she accepted my proposal. The very first thing we did was fall on our knees and ask the Lord to bless our intended union. In about three weeks God sent Mr. Hake another assistant who seemed perfect for the job.

And so on October 7, 1830, we were married.

Our wedding was wonderfully simple. We walked to church. We had no wedding breakfast, but in the afternoon had a blessed service of Holy Communion in the home of Mr. and Mrs. Hake. After that I drove off with my beloved bride in the stagecoach, and the next day we went to work for the Lord.

As simple as our beginning was, and so unlike the habits of most of the world, that's how we have tried to live our whole lives—simple, for Jesus' sake.

Here's what I notice about how God brought me my dear wife:

1. Someone gave me Miss Paget's address.

2. Even though I delayed, I finally went to see her.

3. Miss Paget might have referred me elsewhere to rent a room, but God's hand directed her to send me to Mr. Hake's boarding house.

4. I might have continued in my decision not to marry, but God spoke to me. It seemed that He said to me, "You can tell that Mary is fond of you; you know that you have treated her with kindness and respect and are fond of her; and though it may seem unkind to leave Mr. Hake without an assistant, you ought to propose to Mary."

5. I obeyed. The result has been nothing but one continuous stream of blessing.

Here is one additional word of counsel: To enter into marriage is one of the most important events of one's entire life. You cannot pray too much about this. Our future happiness, our usefulness, and whether we live for God or for ourselves afterward often results from this one important choice. That's why this decision must be made yielded to God and with earnest, deep prayer.

The decision to marry must not be made based on beauty, age, money, or intelligence. Wait upon God. Fix your focus on God and be willing to be guided by Him. The most important characteristic to look for in a companion for life is true godliness. You should be able to observe the person's godly character, *without a shadow of doubt.*

In addition to this, however, compatibility is important. For example, it's not a good idea for an educated man to marry an entirely uneducated woman. No matter how much he may love her, it will lead to unhappy issues.

CRITICAL ILLNESS OF GEORGE MUELLER'S DAUGHTER

In July 1853 God tried my faith in a way I had never experienced before. My beloved daughter and only child, a believer herself for the past seven years, was taken ill on June 20, 1853.

At first it was just a low fever, but then it developed into dreaded typhus. Two weeks later it looked like there was no chance of recovery.

Now was my trial of faith.

But—faith triumphed! My wonderful wife and I did indeed give her up into the hands of God. Truly He sustained us both exceedingly. Even though my only child—whom I loved profoundly—was near death, my soul remained in perfect peace. I knew that my heavenly Father would, of course, do only what was best for her, and for her parents. I was content with that.

She continued to hover near death until July 20, when she began to recover. By August 18 she was so much better that, although she was still very weak, we were able to move her to Clevedon, where she continued to recover.

Parents know what an only child, a much loved child, is and must be to believing parents. Through this entire ordeal I heard my heavenly Father say to me, "Are you willing to give up this child to me?" And my heart responded, *Your will be done. You alone know what is best.*

But as our hearts gave back our own child to Him who had first given her to us, so He gave her back to us again—to live. Psalm 37:4 says, "Delight yourself in the LORD and he will give you the desires of your heart"; and truly the desires of my heart were for my daughter to live, but more than that *to be satisfied with the will of the Lord.* Truly, of all the trials of faith I have ever had to pass through, this one was by far the greatest. By God's abundant mercy I was able to delight myself in the will of God, for I felt perfectly sure that if God took this beloved daughter, it would be because it was best for her parents, best for her, and more for the glory of God than if she lived. Knowing this is what gave my heart that peace—perfect peace. I did not have a moment's anxiety.

I am convinced that every believer who is exercising faith will have this same perfect peace, even in the most trying times.

THE DAILY BREAD

August 3, 1844: We began the day with $3. My soul reached toward heaven and I began to watch expectantly to see how the Lord would provide for us this day, because I knew *for sure* that He would provide. We have had lots of Saturdays when we did not have enough for the day, and God has always provided. And so He will do so this day also.

About 9 o'clock three workers and I began to pray for our needs. While we were still praying, there was a knock on the door and I was informed that someone had come to see me. When we finished praying I went out to discover that someone had brought $6 for the orphans. I began looking to the Lord for more.

August 6, 1844—three days later: The day began without a single penny in my hands. Nothing arrived in the mail. At 10:10 a.m. the courier brought me the daily delivery from the orphanage. Now see how God provides!

In this courier bag there was a note from one of the staff members with $1, stating that this was part of an unexpected gift she had just received.

September 4, 1844: This morning I have just a single penny in my hands. Remember, we have nearly 140 people to feed each day. You, Reader, may have six or eight children to feed; you may think that your wages are small. Or you may be in the middle class, but still straining to make ends meet.

No matter—think of this! Is there any reason you can't do the same thing we're doing? When you worry about how you will buy food for your own family, can you learn from us? Does God love you less than He loves us? Doesn't He love all His children just as much as He loves His one and only begotten Son? In John 17:23 Jesus prays to the Father, "You sent me and have *loved them even as you have loved me*" (emphasis added). Do you think we are better than you?

No! I am just like you—a simple, poor sinner, just like you. Do you think a single person has a claim on God because they are *worthy*? Not at all! It is only the righteousness of the Lord Jesus that makes any of us worthy to receive anything from our heavenly Father. We get it from Him!

Therefore, we pray in our every need, and *you can too*. We ask our Father for every need, and He helps us. Our same Father is willing to help all His children who put their trust in Him.

And so this morning, with the single penny in my pocket, I prayed. A little after 9 o'clock I received $5 from a dear woman. By 11 o'clock the courier bag arrived; it had a note stating that the house needed $5 today.

I had scarcely finished reading this note when someone else came to my door. It was a believer who was in Bristol on other business. He had heard about our orphanages, and was amazed that we were able to manage without any system at all for requesting donations, but instead relied on faith and prayer. He was very moved and gave me $10,000, with a promise for more each year. This was a man whom I had never heard of before today.

THE POOR ARE WITH YOU ALWAYS

February 12, 1845: After sending off the money the orphanages needed for today, I was left with only $4, which is only a fraction of what is needed for one day. So today again there is a fresh need for trusting in the Lord.

In the morning I met with my wife for our usual prayer time together, and today we were joined by her sister. We asked the Lord for many blessings and also that God would provide for our needs. About an hour later I received a letter with a donation of $110, which was a wonderful encouragement to our faith in a God who answers prayer!

I also noted something else. For the past several months I have been increasingly concerned about the needs of so many of my Christian brothers and sisters, many of whom live in poverty. Jesus said, "The poor you will always have with you, and you can help them any time you want" (Mark 14:7), and these words have been stirring in my heart. I have been praying for the poor, and did so again this morning. Today was the coldest morning we have had the whole winter.

During my morning walk (a time I always used for prayer and meditation), I thought how blessed I was. I had plenty of coal to keep me warm, nourishing food, and warm clothing. I wondered how many of God's dear children might not have even these basic necessities, and so I lifted my heart up to God and asked Him to send me more so I could give it to others and show I cared by my actions. Just three hours later I received a $50 donation, earmarked for my own needs.

TALK ABOUT THIS

1. How is Mueller's advice regarding marriage different from the norm today? What does he say is the most important characteristic to look for in a mate?

2. Have you ever known someone who has experienced the loss of a child? Or experienced a traumatic illness? How difficult is it to find God's peace at a time like this? Why was Mueller's experience so different from the norm?

3. How was it possible for Mueller to have peace throughout his daughter's critical illness? What were the "desires of his heart" at this time?

4. Do you think it got easier for Mueller to trust God after living this way for several years? Why or why not?

5. In the "Daily Bread" section, Mueller had $3 and his soul "reached toward heaven" to see how God would provide. If you or I were in that situation, we would probably be looking not toward heaven, but toward any possible earthly means we could think of. Explain the difference.

6. It was common for Mueller to have no money at all (or very little) and yet he began to have a growing concern for "the poor." Does this seem odd to you?

APPLICATION: WHAT IF I...?

1. What if I faced my most trying times with a new determination to trust God, *no matter what*?

2. What if I knew, for sure, that there was no circumstance in the world that could destroy my trust in Jesus? What would that look like? What difference would that make in my life?

3. What if I looked to God to supply my daily bread, and confidently *expected* an answer?

4. What if I cared about the poor and began to pray for ways to help them?

Chapter 11

THREE HUNDRED PEOPLE TO FEED—NO SOURCE OF INCOME

And I Thought I Had Problems!

A CHANGE IN MY MORNING WALK

FEBRUARY 1, 1847: Before breakfast I headed out for my usual early morning walk, but today I took a different direction, sensing God's hand nudging me to do so. As I returned home I met a Christian man whom I used to pass by almost every morning, but had not seen for some time because I had not walked in this direction recently. He stopped me and gave me $10 for the orphans, and then I knew why God had led me to take this path today. We did not have enough in hand yet to meet the needs of the day, so I knew this donation was part of God's provision.

February 4, 1847—three days later: No donations came in yesterday. This morning just before I began my prayer time, I received a $5 donation with a brief note: "From a friend who recently toured the boys' orphanage and was impressed with what she saw." After receiving this, I prayed that God would supply our needs.

Fifteen minutes after praying, a letter arrived with $25. The donor's letter said this was from the proceeds of a strip of land he had just sold to the railroad company. I am amazed at how many different ways God uses to answer our prayers and provide for our needs!

CONTINUED TRIALS OF FAITH AND PATIENCE

October 7, 1852: The work of caring for orphans continues to grow. We are now caring for 330 people, and thus the trials of faith continue.

We have absolutely no guaranteed income at all. We must look to God for every single thing we need. Sometimes the financial needs are actually the smallest part of our needs. All of it, however, *every single need*, we are privileged to bring to the Father, and we are not disappointed.

This evening we only had $40 left in hand for the current expenses. We have not been lacking for the past several months, but are now very needy. We have had greater expenses than usual, and every undesignated gift has been put into the building fund.

And so, it was time for some devoted prayer time.

October 9, 1852—two days later: I have been reading the book of Luke during my Bible reading, and today read the story of the centurion and the raising of the widow's son in chapter seven. Reading about these amazing examples of Jesus' power and ability, I began to pray, *Lord Jesus, You are the same today! You have the same power today as You had back then. You can provide me with the funds needed for Your orphanage work here. Please do so, for the sake of Your name.*

About 30 minutes later, I received $1,150!

The joy that comes from such answers to prayer cannot be described. I was determined to wait on God alone and not do anything that might be construed as manipulating people or events to receive the much-needed funds.

In fact, I have thousands of dollars in the building fund, but I would not touch this money for daily needs because it's already designated for the building fund. I also knew that a $500 gift was promised to us, and for two months now we've been expecting it any day. Knowing about this gift, I might have been tempted to borrow $500 from the building fund and plan to repay it when this gift finally arrived, but I clearly knew that doing this would have been stepping out of God's plan. It is God's work, and it is God who provides for every need.

The very day this $1,150 donation arrived, I had another $500 in my hands that had been given for the building fund. And even though we had such an urgent need, I remained steadfast in my determination not to touch it for our daily needs. I was on my way to the bank to deposit it into the building fund when the $1,150 donation arrived. I knew that I could, and would, wait upon God.

My soul does magnify the Lord for His goodness!

June 13, 1853: We are now very poor. We do, in fact, have a little money but need to buy flour, oatmeal, soap, and pay the workmen for several little repairs around the house. This is all in addition to our regular expenses of about $350 per week. And on Saturday I found that the furnace needs to be repaired, which will probably cost $125. All totaled, it looks like we need about $500 for these extra expenses.

I was aware that humanly speaking, I could see no prospects whatsoever for receiving this extra money—not even $5, let alone $500. And today is Monday; we usually receive very little on Mondays.

As I walked to the orphanage this morning, I was praying as usual. I specifically told the Lord that even though today was Monday, He could send me a large donation.

And so it was! I received $1,505 to be used wherever it's needed.

The joy I had cannot be described. I paced back and forth in my room for a very long time, tears of joy and gratitude to God raining down my cheeks. I was filled with praise and continued for some time magnifying the Lord for His amazing goodness and surrendering myself again, with all my heart, to Him.

God, You can use me in any way You need me.

I don't know if I have ever felt the kindness of the Lord more than today.

November 9, 1853: We are again at a point of very great need. The Lord tries our faith and patience. This afternoon a couple stopped in to see me at the new orphanage. After spending a few minutes with them, she gave me $5, which a friend of hers had sent. She herself gave me $5 for my own personal support, and another $5 for the building fund. Her husband gave me $25 for the orphanage and $25 for missionary support.

These unexpected gifts greatly encouraged me, and I now am looking for and expecting more from God.

November 12, 1853: This evening as I was praying for funds, a package arrived with $50. What an encouragement to my spirit!

July 12, 1854: I am down to just $150; only about $750 has come in during the past thirty days. We are facing some very heavy expenses.

This morning I was reading through the book of Proverbs, and came to 22:19, "So that your trust may be in the LORD," and I prayed to the Lord, *Lord, I do trust in You, but would You now please help me? I am really in need; would you help me take care of all of these expenses?*

The morning's mail brought me a check for $500, to be used "wherever there is need."

October 17, 1854: This morning during family Bible reading and prayer, we came to Exodus 5. We noticed that just before the Hebrews were delivered out of Egypt, their trials were greater than ever. They not only had to make the same number of bricks per day, but now they had to gather their own straw because none would be provided for them. And so I observed that the same is often true today. Just before help comes, God's children are often brought to greater trials than ever before.

Immediately after we finished family prayers, we learned that today's mail had not brought us a single penny, though we desperately needed funds. In fact, very little had come in for the last three days. I realized that reading Exodus 5 was the perfect reading for today; now it was time to practice this truth.

Throughout the whole long day, nothing was received. Evening came and I had my usual prayer with my wife and then we left the orphanage for home.

When we arrived home at 9:00 p.m., we found that $25 had come for the building fund and that $40 had come in for the distribution of Bibles and tracts. This called for thanksgiving. A little later someone stopped by with a $5 gift for the orphans and $1,000 for the support of foreign missionaries. He explained that the large gift was from an elderly woman; the $1,000 was her entire life savings. She had just learned she was to receive a small monthly distribution, and since it would be enough for her to live on, she felt compelled to give her life savings for missions.

No date provided: We have been praying specifically that the Lord would send us funds for the support of missionaries. I knew they were really in need and had prayed just two hours earlier for this very thing! I immediately prepared $200 to send to the missionaries in British Guiana and promptly mailed it. I wish I could have sent more, but this is all I have.

ARE YOU PREPARED FOR ETERNITY?

Today as I reviewed my accounting books, I noticed how many of our previous donors have passed from earth to eternity. It made me think that my time—and yours—will also come soon.

Are you ready for eternity?

I want to gently press this question upon you. Don't put it aside. Nothing is more important for you to think about than this. Every other pressing matter, every important item on your to-do list doesn't even matter compared to this.

Do you want to know how to be prepared for eternity? Do you want to know how to be saved? The answer is: believe in the Lord Jesus, trust in Him, and depend on Him alone for the salvation of your soul. He was punished by God so that we who were guilty of sin might not be punished, if we just believe in

Him. He fulfilled the law of God and was obedient even unto death so that we disobedient, guilty sinners, if we believe in Him, might be made righteous by God.

Think carefully about this. If you have never really thought about it, think hard. Think now. There's only one way to be forgiven for our sins and be at peace with God and that's by putting your faith in the Lord Jesus. That's it! That's the only way. When we do this, we become the children of God; we have God as our Father. And as His children we can now come to Him for all the earthly and spiritual blessings we need.

If you do this you can have answers to your prayers just like the ones you read about here in this book—and even more!

It may be true that only a few of God's children are called to serve Him by establishing and operating orphanages. But all of you are definitely called to trust God, to rely on Him in your daily life. No matter what your circumstances, you need to trust God, apply the Word of God, faith, and prayer to those circumstances, to your family, job, health, and every need.

You see how *we* do it! With God's help, in some small measure, we seek to apply the truths of the Bible, faith, and prayer to every part of our lives.

Try it out! If you have never tried trusting God—try it; and you will see how happy a life it is!

Truly I prefer this life by far. Even though my life has almost constant trials, it is filled with constant inner peace. My inner peace is so much better than a life with outward peace and quietness. I only have to roll all my cares upon my heavenly Father. When I do this I find that I become increasingly acquainted with Him. Truly nothing compares with that closeness. When I face these daily trials, they lead me to constant proofs of His faithfulness, His wisdom, His love, His power, and His overruling providence.

Talk About This

1. Have you ever had an unexpected change of plans or a spontaneous thought to do something out-of-the-ordinary, only to discover later that God planned it for His purposes? Share.

2. Have you ever worried about how you would feed your own family? Or pay all your bills? How does your experience compare with Mueller's attitude when he had 330 people to feed and no income?

3. Mueller states that he desperately needed money for daily needs, yet he would not touch money he had readily available in the building fund. Why? What would have happened if he had borrowed needed funds? Do you agree with him? Why or why not? What would you do?

4. Are you surprised that, with God in charge, Mueller is so very poor—so often? Why do you think this is? How does this compare with "prosperity preachers" and writers?

APPLICATION: WHAT IF I...?

1. What if I embraced the next unexpected change that came my way and looked for the hand of God in it?

2. What if I never again worried about how I was going to pay my bills? Is that even possible?

3. What if I became so enthralled with a new life lived by a radical faith and absolute trust in God to provide and care for me, that I longed for others to have it too? How would that be different from my current life?

Chapter 12

FORTY YEARS AND COUNTING—WHAT HAS CHANGED?

SEPTEMBER 6, 1854: Today I received $250; half of it is to be used for missions and the other half as I think best. I used this second half for the needs of the orphans—what a precious answer to prayer! For the past two weeks we have been coming to the Lord daily for our daily needs. It is also a precious provision for the missionaries we support. Prior to this donation, I had nothing to send them.

It occurs to me to reflect on some basic truths about our work:

1. If anyone reads this journal and sees how low our funds have been depleted so often, and assumes that the orphans, therefore, have had to do without necessities, I want to set the record straight. There has never been one time since this work was begun that a single meal was missed. The children have had good, nourishing food in sufficient quantity; they have never needed clothes; indeed, there has never been a single need that has gone lacking. God has sent me the means to provide them with everything they needed.

2. Not one time since the orphan work began have I asked a single human being for any help for this

work. And yet, without being asked, donations have come in from all over the world, simply in answer to prayer. Frequently donations have come in at a time when we had the greatest need.

1859: Every Wednesday evening I meet with the staff for prayer. I pray several times each day, at specific times. During these prayers I seek to bring the work before God, laying before Him fifty or more matters that are at hand, and thus I obtain His blessing. I ask no human being for help concerning the work.

Even if I could get $50,000 from someone just by asking, by God's grace I would not ask. Do you know why? It's because I have cheerfully dedicated my whole life to find a clear, concrete, visible way to demonstrate to the world and to the church an undeniable demonstration that it makes perfect sense to trust in God! It is my privilege to wait upon God. He is the same living God today as He ever was, and He is revealed throughout the Holy Scriptures. If we know Him and are reconciled to Him through faith in the Lord Jesus, if we ask Him in Jesus' name for needs that are according to His will, He will surely give them to us, in His own time, provided that we believe He will.

God has never, ever failed me. For forty years I have proved His faithfulness.

The Lord Is the Rock Eternal

November 9, 1861: Saturday evening. When the week began, I received only $20 in the mail. As I began my Bible reading time, I came to Isaiah 26:4 "Trust in the LORD forever, for the LORD, the LORD, is the Rock eternal." I laid my Bible aside and fell on my knees. *Lord, I do believe that you are the eternal Rock. You are the source of rock-solid strength and I trust You. Help me, O Lord, to trust in You forever. Please give me* *more donations today and more this week, even though so little has come in so far.*

Later that same day, I received $50, $25, and $10 from three different donors; and by the end of the week a total of $2,285 had come in! God has again proved Himself to be the eternal Rock!

Reader, I want you to trust in the Lord the same way I do. If you are not in the habit of doing so already, do it now! You will find how blessed it is, just as I have many thousands of times. If, however, you are stumbling through life and are careless about your soul or don't know about God and His Son, Jesus, then the first (and most important) thing you should do is trust in the Lord Jesus for the salvation of your soul, have your sins forgiven, and be reconciled to God.

Jesus Christ, the Same Yesterday, Today, and Forever

May 26, 1861: At the close of the period, I find that our total expenses for everything are $123,500, or $338 per day. During the coming year I expect the expenses to be considerably greater. But God, who has always helped me these many years, will help me in the future also.

You see by now how the Lord helps us year after year. He is faithful. The expenses increase every year because the operations have been enlarged each year, but He never fails us.

I can imagine that someone might ask, "What would you do if God failed to help you?"

I am glad to answer: it is just *not possible* for God to fail! As long as we trust Him and do not live in sin, He is faithful to answer prayer and provide for us.

However, if we forsake Him, the fountain of living waters, and take off on our own by trusting in our own flesh, we would be like broken jugs that cannot hold water. If we began to live in sin, then yes—it would be foolish to call on Him for help, even if we still profess to trust in Him. "If I had cherished sin in my heart, the Lord would not have listened" (Ps. 66:18).

By God's grace, I have been able to continue trusting in Him alone; and even though I am weak in many ways, still, by God's grace, I have been able to walk uprightly, hating sin and loving holiness. The longing of my heart is to be more and more like Jesus.

November 21, 1868: Each new day we make our requests known before Him. Our expenses have been $500 per day for several years now, but even with such high expenses, He has never failed us. In some ways we have been like the "burning bush in the wilderness" and yet not consumed. And still we trust in God! Our spirits remain high even though we know our expenses will continue to go up each year.

If every person who follows Christ only knew the blessings of truly looking to God alone, trusting in Him alone, they would soon see how refreshing it is! How entirely beyond disappointment! Unbelievers may never understand our work; but if we work for God, it doesn't matter if anyone understands—God does!

Friends may lose their ability to help us even if they fervently want to, but God never changes—He is the infinitely rich One.

Friends may change their mind and decide to send their support to other causes; but He is able to send us new support. Even if our needs multiply a million times over, He can supply everything that could possibly be needed, and He does it with delight! He has *no limits* at all.

Any place on earth where His will is being done and where He is confided in, He supplies the needs.

Friends may die, and so we lose their support, but He lives forever. He cannot die. We trust in the living God alone. Not one, not two, not even five or ten, but many, many more people who once helped us with generous donations have eventually died; but have our operations been stopped because of that?

No! And why is that? It is because I trust in God, and in God alone.

PREPARED FOR TRIALS OF FAITH

July 28, 1874: For many months now it seems to me that the Lord intends to bring us back to where we started—when we looked to Him day by day for our supplies. From August 1838 to April 1849, it was like that almost without exception; we never had more in hand than enough for the day, and yet God always provided. Sometimes we had to look to God from one meal to the next.

Because our work is now twenty times larger than it was then, this *seems like* a very great difficulty. Although our purchases are now made wholesale, I am still comforted by the knowledge that God knows all about it; and if He knows this is the way to glorify His name, then that's exactly what I want. God alone knows what will show His church, and unbelievers, that it is His own hand that provides for us. So by His grace I am willing to go this way and continue this way to the very end. *God decides.*

Our funds continue to go out as fast as they come in. God, our infinitely rich Treasurer, continues to provide. And this is what gives me peace!

At present we need $220,000 per year to maintain our operations, but if it pleases Him to have me do in the evening of my life what I did during the early dawn years, then that's exactly what I'll do. I am prepared for it and gladly face these trials of faith. Whatever glorifies God and helps the church and unbelievers!

I have thought about this often lately. I now have 2,100 people to feed every day, and no money at all. I also have 189 missionaries that I support and no money in hand for them. And I now have one hundred schools with about nine hundred students in them that must be entirely supported and don't have a cent for them. In addition, I always send out four million tracts and tens of thousands of Bibles each year; this fund is also depleted.

As I write this and face the reality of these numbers, here's what I think. God, who has raised up this work through me; God, who has led me to enlarge the work each year; God, who has always been the Provider for forty years now—this same God will still help! He will not leave me confused or abandoned, because I rely on Him. And so, I commit the whole work to Him. He will provide me with what I need, just as He has these past forty years, even though I have no idea where that help will come from.

When I came home last evening, I found several letters with donations totaling $1,000. One was from a foreign missionary that we support who had just inherited some funds. This morning I received another $120. Heading into the afternoon prayer time with a group of staff workers, we gave thanks for this provision and prayed for spiritual blessings, needed rain, and health of the staff. We also asked God to send us more donations.

When we finished praying, someone handed me a letter with a $375 donation. What an immediate answer to our prayers!

August 12, 1874: The income for this whole week has been $4,500.

September 16, 1874: Today as we prayed for funds, I specifically asked that God would send us some of the expected gifts that we know are coming from deceased people's estates. These take some time to settle and disburse funds, and I prayed that the funds would be released soon. Immediately after this prayer, I received a gift of $9,000 from one of the estates.

September 23, 1874: Today's income was $26,850, most of it from a single donor. The Lord be praised!

TALK ABOUT THIS

1. Forty years and counting—what has changed? What is still the same?

2. Mueller often mentions that he prays regularly with his wife, with colleagues, or with the staff. How important is it to Mueller to pray with others? Why?

3. Mueller states, "If we know Him and are reconciled to Him through faith in the Lord Jesus, if we ask in Jesus' name for needs that are according to His will, He will surely give them to us, in His time, provided that we believe He will." This sentence includes some very specific conditions. What are they? Do you think all are important?

4. Mueller writes, "As I began my Bible reading time, I came to..." Share with the class what you are reading in your personal Bible reading time. Share if you have recently sensed God speaking directly to you through your Bible reading.

5. Mueller writes, "Reader, I want you to trust in the Lord the same way I do. If you are not in the habit of doing so already, do it now!" Do you think trusting in the Lord is a *habit*? Is *not* trusting in God also a habit?

6. Mueller details the numbers of people he is now supporting. Keep in mind his bank balance and his level of peace while supporting this many. Discuss.

7. Do you think keeping a prayer journal is a good idea?

8. Mueller writes, "Any place on earth where His will is being done and where He is confided in, He supplies the needs." Do you agree? Have you ever seen evidence of this?

APPLICATION: WHAT IF I...?

1. What if I prayed with my spouse, my accountability partner, my staff, or my small group at regular, appointed times?

2. What if I had the same amount of faith every day, no matter how my circumstances might change?

3. What if I resolved to tell only God (and no person) the next time I had a concrete need that I had no way of meeting on my own?

Chapter 13

MUELLER'S LAST YEARS
AND DEPARTURE

Marting 27, 1881: Today we have no money in hand at all. We have spent nearly $7,000 during the past month.

What should we do now? With no money, what should we do?

Well, we knew exactly what to do! We did what we have done for forty-seven years—we went on our knees before God. Again and again, we placed our requests before God.

My wife and I are in the United States; and even here, we love our habitual daily time of prayer. With the deep needs now before us, we stop four, five, or six more times in our day for heartfelt prayer. We make our requests known to our heavenly Father and are assured that help will come.

I know this plan may seem foolish to some, be ridiculed by others, and be considered irrational by others, but without fail, we have found prayer and faith to be our complete, dependable solution. Now that we have fifty years' experience with this plan, we can heartily declare that God is always faithful. We will continue waiting on Him so that we can show an ungodly world and a doubting church that the living God is still able and willing to answer prayer, and that it is the joy of His heart to listen to the prayers of His children.

Psalm 9:10 says, "Those who know your name will trust in you, for you, Lord, have never forsaken those who seek you." We know Him and do, therefore, put our trust in Him.

April 27, 1881: On March 27 we had no funds in hand. However, in the past month we have been helped in answer to prayer and have been supplied with all we needed, even though our needs totaled $5,000. Today we even have $115 left.

April 29, 1881: A dear Christian friend, who, constrained by the love of Christ to lay up her treasures in heaven, has received an inheritance and sent us $2,500, keeping very little of it for herself.

July 28, 1881: Lately the income has been about one-third of what we need for normal operations. Consequently, our fund for support of the orphans is near zero. On the face of it, it appears that we will have to shut down the work.

But I believe the Lord will help and that we will not be put to shame. I do not think it's God's plan to shut down any of this work; it is *His* work! I am fully expecting help and am writing this down for the glory of God, so that when help arrives, it is already recorded here that I expected it. I do this for the encouragement of God's children. We shall see what the results will be.

We have not been this poor for seven years, but I have no doubt that God will provide. We will meet our expenses.

August 15, 1881: The balance on hand is now only $1,675— less than it has been for a long time. This is the amount we have to feed 2,100 people. It is only enough for about four and one-half days, but our eyes are on the Lord. I look to my heavenly Father.

Our total income received today is $140.

August 22, 1881: Settlement on an estate was finally completed after many years and payments disbursed; we received $5,000 from it, as an answer to many prayers.

February 26, 1882: Balance on hand today is $485, which is $120 more than the average expenses of a single day.

March 2, 1882: Our prayers lately are simple: "Give us *this day* our *daily* bread." For some time now, it has been like that— praying for each day's needs, but God has not failed us.

April 20, 1882: Just when we were at our greatest need, we received $500 with the following note: "The enclosed donation was intended to be part of my will, but I am sending it to you now."

June 3, 1882: Received a wonderful gift of $2,500. I saw it as a sign from God, and knew that more would come.

October 21, 1882: Received another $5,000. God, in answer to our prayers, spoke to this dear donor and prompted him to send us more than ever. I observe that God always gives us proof. During the previous year when we were so very low on funds, it was just so we could be tested and learn to trust Him more. God was not indicating that He was done with us. For me, I *expect* more help from God. I have never been disappointed.

August 17, 1883: By this afternoon our balance reached $51. Think of this! We have 2,100 people to provide for, and all we have is $51. We are exactly where we were forty-six years ago. God is our banker. In Him we trust and on Him we draw by faith.

This evening, we received $150. On Monday we received $645 but had to pay out $300. On Tuesday we received $1,475, but had to pay out $900.

It seems to please God to vary the sources from which we receive funds. He does this so that we never become dependent on a single source and don't look to an earthly source to meet our needs. We have learned to keep our eyes fixed on Him. By His grace we have done so and our hearts are kept in peace.

June 7, 1884: We have $205 on hand—about half what is needed for one day's operation. We also learned that we needed $10,000 to repair our sewer system and have no funds for such an expense.

At just the right time, we received $55,170—the largest donation I have ever received at one time. It was a settlement from an estate that had taken six years to settle. I had prayed for its release for six years, always believing that God would release it in His own time (which is *always* the best).

I have prayed many times for estates to settle and pay disbursements that were left to us, and now again, I see that God's timing is perfect.

Excerpt from the 54th Annual Report (1893)

The readers of the last report may remember some of the trials we had from May 26, 1892, to May 16, 1893, but we trusted in God. With unshaken confidence we looked to Him, and we expected that somehow God would help. This is our attitude, and my heart continued to be at peace, knowing that all of this was being permitted by God Himself and would end up being a blessing for thousands who would read about it later. I have already seen how it encouraged the faith of our own staff, and they are the very ones who are on the front lines, watching the hand of God day by day.

August 30, 1892: This evening, while reading in the Psalms, I came again to Psalm 81:10 and remembered that it was this very verse that started this whole thing. I read it on December 4, 1835, and the Holy Spirit used this verse to speak to me. From that moment God has led me to establish the greatest orphanage in the world, but I thought also what blessings have come from it to tens of thousands of believers and unbelievers all over the world.

I put aside my Bible and fell on my knees. I asked God to graciously repeat His former kindness and supply me again more abundantly with means. And in less than one-half hour, I received $250; by the end of the day, the total was $760.

November 11, 1892: The early mail delivery brought only $45, but by the end of the day, I had $1,000. I am never discouraged when the donations are small; I remind myself (and my staff), "More prayer, more patience, and more exercise of faith will bring greater blessing." In my experience, for all sixty-three years since I began this life of entire dependence on God for everything, I find this to be true.

March 1, 1893: The income for this week was $465, which is about one-sixth what is needed, but the great trial of our faith will soon be over.

March 4, 1893—three days later: *This very day*, God began to answer our prayers. We have received a very good offer on the land we have to sell—an incredible $5,000 per acre! And yet, the beginning of the day was darker than ever by human appearances; but we trusted God for help. The early mail delivery brought us only $20, and even by the end of the day, the total was just $40, far short of the $450 needed per day.

But now God has helped us. This evening we sold 10.4 acres of land at $5,000 per acre; we shall receive $52,000 total for this one field. The contract was signed at 8 o'clock this evening.

GEORGE MUELLER'S DEPARTURE
TO BE WITH CHRIST

Editor's note: On the evening of Wednesday, March 9, 1898, George Mueller took part in the usual prayer meeting held at orphanage number three, and returned to his home for the evening. Early the following morning, he breathed his last, fulfilling his dream "to depart and be with Christ."

George Mueller had served God faithfully for sixty-four years. During the course of his lifetime, he handled more than $8 million; and yet, at his death, his own worldly possessions were valued at about $800.

TALK ABOUT THIS

1. How is Mueller's writing similar and different from "positive thinking" writers? Compare and contrast.

2. What are some reasons God allows delays?

3. Mueller reflects on why he thinks they were "so very low on funds." What were his thoughts? Compare this with your own thoughts during similar times.

4. Do you think Mueller had any idea of the impact he would eventually make on the world when he started out?

APPLICATION: WHAT IF I...?

1. What if I began keeping a prayer journal?

2. What if I viewed "delays" in answered prayer differently?

3. What if I read from the Bible regularly, asking God to teach me each time?

4. What if I read through the entire Bible?

You Want Answers to Your Prayers?

Here Are Five Conditions:

1. Entire dependence on the Lord Jesus Christ. His merits and intervention are the only basis for any claim to blessings. (See John 14:13–14; 15:16.)

2. Separation from all known sin. Psalm 66:18: "If I had cherished sin in my heart, the Lord would not have listened."

3. Faith in God's Word. If I don't believe what God says, I imply that God is a liar and perjurer. Hebrews 11:6: "And without faith it is impossible to please God, because anyone who comes to him must believe that he exists and that he rewards those who earnestly seek him." (See also vv. 13–20.)

4. Ask according to His will. Our motives must be godly. We must not seek any gift from God just to satisfy our own lusts. (See 1 John 5:14; James 4:3.)

5. Persistence in prayer. We must wait on God and wait for God. (See James 5:7; Luke 18:1–8.)

How to Know God's Will
The Mueller Method

FIRST I SEEK to get my heart into such a state that it has no will of its own in regard to the matter at hand. Ninety percent of the trouble with people generally is right here. Ninety percent of the difficulties are overcome when our hearts are ready to do the Lord's will, *whatever it may be.* When you are truly in this state of totally seeking only God's will, you are usually very close to the knowledge of what His will is. *God, whatever You tell me to do, I'll do it.*

Having first done this, I do not leave the result to feelings or simple impression. If I did that, I would be susceptible to great delusions.

Next, I seek the will of the Spirit of God through reading the Bible. The Spirit and the Word must be combined. If I look to the Spirit alone without reading the Word, I lay myself open to great delusions. When the Holy Spirit guides us, He does it according to the Scriptures and never contrary to them. God never contradicts Himself.

Next, I take into account providential circumstances. As I pray, I look for doors that open and watch for doors that close. These often plainly indicate God's will in connection with His Word and Spirit.

I then ask God in prayer to reveal His will to me correctly.

Thus through prayer, the study of the Word, and personal reflection, I come to a deliberate judgment according to the best of my ability and knowledge. If my mind is then at peace and continues so after two or three more times of prayer, I proceed accordingly.

I have found this method is always effective for major as well as minor things.

READING THE BIBLE
COVER TO COVER

*G*EORGE *M*UELLER WAS *a man of the Bible. Early in his life he wrote the following:*
Like so many young believers, I fell into the snare of reading religious books rather than the Bible itself. I read Christian tracts, missionary papers, sermons, and biographies of godly people. I especially liked reading good biographies.

If this reading had steered me toward more Bible reading, or if I had not read too much from them (instead of the Bible), they might have been good for me. I had never developed the habit of reading the Holy Scriptures.

At school we occasionally read a little from the Bible; but after leaving school, I never touched it. I never read one single chapter of it as far as I remember, until it pleased God to stir my heart.

Think of it! God Himself has condescended to become an author, and I am ignorant about it! It is filled with information I need to know; it is filled with knowledge of how to find true happiness. You would think I would read it again and again. I should read it earnestly, prayerfully, and with meditation.

I should make it a practice to do this all the days of my life.

I was aware that I knew almost nothing about it; yet I didn't read it. My ignorance of God's Word, difficulty in understanding it, and lack of enjoyment from it made me lazy. Now I realize that reading it prayerfully makes all the difference! Reading it prayerfully not only helped me understand it, but also increased my delight!

Instead, for the first four years of my Christian life, I read works of uninspired men rather than the inspired words of God. The consequences were predictable: I remained an infant in knowledge and grace. I was so ignorant that I did not even know the fundamental points of our holy faith! And this lack of knowledge, sadly, kept me back from walking steadily in God's path.

It is the truth that sets us free! (See John 8:31–32.)

The truth delivers us from the slavery of lusts of the flesh, lusts of the eyes, and the pride of life. The Word proves it. The experience of other believers proves it. And my own experience now proves it. When I finally came to the Scriptures in August 1829, my life and my walk became very different. Even though I still fall very short of what I could be and ought to be, still, by the grace of God, I have been able to live much nearer to Him than before.

If you are reading this and recognize that you are one of those who prefers other books to the Holy Scriptures, if you enjoy the writings of people much more than the Word of God, let my own loss be a warning for you. I shall consider this book to have done a lot of harm, *if* reading it leads you to neglect your own Bible reading.

I almost hesitate to publish this book for fear that it will only add to the distraction of people reading my words instead of God's words. I pray that you will allow my story to lead you straight to the Bible. Let my mistakes benefit you.

Here is how I advise you to read Scripture:

1. Settle it in your own mind that God alone, by His Spirit, can teach you; and therefore, look to God for blessings as you read.

2. Settle it in your mind that although the Holy Spirit is the *best* and *sufficient* teacher, He does not

always do so immediately. He does not operate on our timetable. We may have to stay prayerfully in meditation, asking Him for meaning of some passages. He will surely teach us if we are truly seeking for His light. Be patient. Look for what will glorify God.

3. It is immensely important that we read a portion of the Old and a portion of the New Testament every day, beginning where we left off the day before. This is important:

   a. Because it throws light upon the connection. If we jump around the Bible, it will be utterly impossible to ever understand much of the Scriptures.

   b. Because while we live in these human bodies, we need the whole variety that is found in the whole Bible.

   c. For the glory of God. If we leave out some chapters here and there, we are saying, in effect, that some portions are better than others, or that there are some parts of revealed truth that are not important, or even not necessary. Are we to censor God?

   d. Because reading the entire Bible may keep us from erroneous views. It is only in reading through the whole Bible that we are able to see the meaning of the whole. This also keeps us from putting too much emphasis on certain favorite views.

   e. The Scriptures contain the whole revealed will of God, and therefore, we ought to seek to read through the whole book from time to time. I know there are many believers who have never even once read the entire Bible, and yet by reading just a little every day, they can accomplish this in just a few months.

f. It is also very important to meditate on what we read. If we do this, we will find that a small portion of what we just read will stay with us the entire day. We may meditate on a portion of one of the gospels, or an epistle every day.

We may learn a lot from various Bible commentaries, but these fill the *head* with thoughts; when we read the Bible, the Spirit teaches us and the *heart* is filled. The former generally puffs up and is often refuted by another commentator with a different opinion. The latter kind of knowledge generally humbles, gives joy, leads us nearer to God, and is not easily reasoned away since we obtain it straight from God.

NOTES

INTRODUCTION
1. Author's paraphrase of ubiquitous old folk tale describing Mueller's ministry.

CHAPTER 9
Missions
1. Hudson Taylor, *China's Millions* (Charleston, SC: Nabo Press, 2009).

ABOUT THE AUTHOR

CINDY MALLIN IS FIRST OF ALL a joyful follower of Christ! After raising three children (now all grown), and homeschooling them during their early years, she is now a grandmother of five little ones. She is blessed with an incredibly happy marriage of three years to Mickey, a wonderful Jewish man who gave his heart to Jesus four years ago and never looked back.

Born and raised in the hills of Pennsylvania, Cindy first came to faith in Christ as a teenager in a very poor, large family with no spiritual heritage and no church background. Always an avid reader, good books became her lifeline, and forty-five years ago, George Mueller became one of her teachers. Reading his story changed her life.

A casual freelance writer for some thirty years, Cindy wrote and published several magazine articles, especially while home raising young children. Later corporate jobs included heading up the local offices of a state representative, serving as operations manager for a small law firm, and executive assistant to the district manager of a global company. Once the children were all launched, she returned to school to complete her bachelor's degree, earning a BS from Roberts Wesleyan College.

These days she enjoys working from home, with husband Mickey, in their real estate investment business and managing rental homes in the Orlando, Florida, area. They enjoy reading good books together, taking walks, and ballroom dancing.

Contact the Author

Cindy welcomes opportunities to speak to
your group and invites your comments and
feedback. You can write to her at:
Cindy@CindyMallin.com